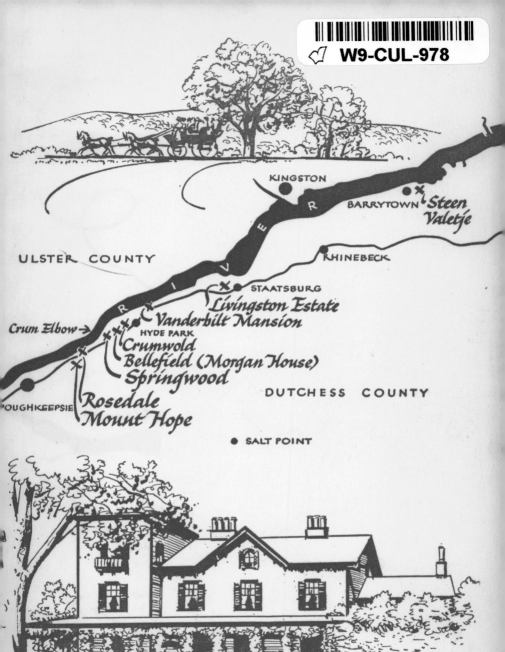

KINGSTON

BARRYTOWN ✗ *Steen Valetje*

R I V E R

ULSTER COUNTY

RHINEBECK

✗ STAATSBURG

Livingston Estate

Vanderbilt Mansion

Crum Elbow →

HYDE PARK

Crumwold

Bellefield (Morgan House)

Springwood

DUTCHESS COUNTY

POUGHKEEPSIE

Rosedale

Mount Hope

● SALT POINT

The Roosevelt House

The House at
HYDE PARK

To fine friends, with the
hope that some of these early
Roosevelt accounts and recipes
may interest you and remind
you of old neighbors, affectionately —
Iney and Doc

The House at
HYDE PARK

BY CLARA AND HARDY STEEHOLM

TOGETHER WITH

Sara Delano Roosevelt's
HOUSEHOLD BOOK

NEW YORK

Published by The Viking Press

1950

PRINTED IN U.S.A. BY H. WOLFF BOOK MANUFACTURING CO.

TABLE OF CONTENTS

LIST OF ILLUSTRATIONS

(*following page 136*)

The Delano and Roosevelt Families

MENTIONED IN *The House at Hyde Park*

WARREN DELANO II (1809–1898) m. Catherine Lyman (1825–1896)
Their children were:
  Susan (1844–1846)
  Louise (1846–1869)
  Deborah [Dora] (1847–1941) m. (1) William Forbes, (2) his brother
      Paul R. Forbes
  Annie Lyman (1849–1926) m. Frederick Delano Hitch
  Warren III (1850–1851)
  Warren III (1852–1920) m. Jennie Walters
  Sara [Sallie] (1854–1941) m. 1880 James Roosevelt (1828–1900)
    Their son Franklin Delano Roosevelt (1882–1945)
  Philippe (1857–1881)
  Katherine [Kassie] (1860–) m. (1) C. A. Robbins, (2) H. Price Collier
  Frederic Adrian (1863–) m. Matilda Peasley
  Laura (1864–1884)

ISAAC ROOSEVELT I ["The Patriot"] (1726–1794) m. Cornelia Hoffman
  Their son James I (1760–1847) m. (1) Maria Eliza Walton, (2) Cath-
      erine Eliza Barclay, (3) Harriet Howland
    His son by his first marriage Isaac II (1790–1863), m. Mary Rebecca
        Aspinwall [daughter of his stepmother's sister Susan How-
        land]
      Their sons: James II (1828–1900) m. (1) Rebecca Howland [daugh-
          ter of his mother's uncle Gardiner Greene Howland],
          (2) Sara Delano
          John Aspinwall (1840–1909) m. Ellen Murray Crosby
        The son of James II and Rebecca Howland was James Roosevelt
            Roosevelt ["Rosy"]
        The son of James II and Sara Delano was Franklin Delano Roose-
            velt

viii   *The Delano and Roosevelt Families*

THEODORE ROOSEVELT *Senior* [fourth cousin to James Roosevelt II] (1831–1878) m. Martha Bulloch

Their children were:

Anna ["Bammie," a close friend of Sara Delano Roosevelt] (1855–1932) m. W. S. Cowles

Theodore *Junior* (1858–1919) President of the United States

Elliott (1860–1894) m. Anna Hall

  Their daughter Anna Eleanor m. Franklin Delano Roosevelt

Corinne (1861–1933) m. Douglas Robinson

  Their son Theodore Douglas m. Helen Roosevelt, daughter of "Rosy," half-brother of Franklin Delano Roosevelt

The House at
HYDE PARK

I

The Household Book

SARA DELANO ROOSEVELT'S name is one which works a kind of magic. She was the mother of our most controversial president, the man who held that office longer than anyone else. In her home he grew up, by her personality his own character was vitally influenced. She and her life have become significant to all of us. Her background, her way of thought, her house, the things that caught her interest, hold ours too.

Since her home at Hyde Park, just north of Poughkeepsie on the Hudson, became a National Historic Site, thousands upon thousands of Americans have walked through it and peered into her rooms. What was it like during her lifetime? they wonder. What was it like when Franklin Roosevelt was a boy? What kind of people were the Roosevelts, and what was the nature of that Hudson Valley life, so remote from us today?

A small notebook of 176 pages, measuring scarcely six by eight inches, holds some of the answers. Sara Roosevelt kept it in her own slanting hand, beginning in the year before she was married. It was discovered in her desk some time after her death and is now preserved in the Roosevelt Family Archives at Hyde Park. No one can look at it today without savoring some of the homely details of that life.

It lists cooking recipes and household hints, home reme-

dies for illness, and farm directions, most of them carefully
credited to the donor, and dated. For want of any precise
title, it has been called Mrs. Roosevelt's "Household Book."
It emerges from the obscurity of her private papers as one
of the authentic guides to life in the Hyde Park house as it
flowed on for half a century.

We can picture her as the young wife of the middle-aged
James Roosevelt, and later as widow and matriarch, sitting
in the ground-floor room now known as the Snuggery, her
special little room, which was part of the South Parlor before the house was remodeled in 1915. Here she had her
own desk and later her own radio. Here she kept her accounts and interviewed the staff of servants; she would sit
here in the morning, dealing with household matters, planning the meals for the family and for the special occasions
which multiplied as the years went on. Her Household
Book was constantly at hand. The entries were not system-
atic; she apparently opened it at random and used the first
blank page that she turned to. But there is testimony to her
dependence on it in the fact that when it was half full she
herself prepared a careful index of its contents, page by page,
so that she could find her way in it.

The first entry was made in 1879, the year the blank book
was given to her by her beloved Aunt Sarah; the latest iden-
tifiable date is 1931—but that is not the last entry in the
book. She had written on the back page in 1881, long before
the rest had begun to be filled, the "List for layette" which
her friend Marian Low had given her. In the margin of that
same page she had confided, in French, a note which would
not then have seemed proper to her to write in English,
even in her private notebook: *"Pour compter les jours . . ."*

Her son was born a few months later. It is safe to suppose
that this was the first written reference to his individual existence.

With the Household Book in hand, it is possible to re-create much of the rich structure of Hudson River society in the closing decades of the last century. When you know what people like to eat, you learn a good deal about them; when you find out where they went and when, another vista is opened to you. And when you learn who were their servants, their nurses, their family physicians, their friends and intimate associates, you are rewarded with a good straight look at the pattern of their personalities. In such recipes as the one for oyster toast, with its exhortation to "Eat in solemn silence and wash down with a glass of brown sherry," one can sense a statelier and more expansive home life than our own. And the common recurrence of such delectables as Moonshines, Pan Dowdy, Laplanders, Chutney, and Mont Blanc reminds us how the homely and the cosmopolitan still blended in that day.

The notebook was never intended to be more than Mrs. Roosevelt's private jottings on matters of farm and household interest. But the identification of initials alone sheds light. The entries obtained from S. A. D., A. L. D. H., and Harriet Wood bring sharply into focus the strong bond between Mrs. Roosevelt, her father's sister Sarah Alvey Delano, and her own sister Annie Lyman Delano Hitch, and lead us to want to know more about the Delanos at Algonac down the river.

The references to Mother Roosevelt and Rosedale throw the mild shadow of Dr. Isaac Roosevelt, Franklin's grandfather, upon the screen of history and make his story vital to our clear understanding of how the Roosevelts came to make Hyde Park their home.

The explanation of how a railroad-car porter named William Yapp gave Mrs. Roosevelt a recipe for "egg bread" leads directly to Franklin's father, James, and his various business interests; and the egg-nog recipe from J. R. calls with certainty for our better knowledge of the man whom Sara Delano married.

On nearly every page of the Household Book there are clues which lead us to acquaintanceship with many of the people who were important to Sara Roosevelt and her son. The handwriting in this informal notebook, still clear and legible, adds reality to the great tapestry of color and incident which has already begun to be woven as a background for the figure of Franklin D. Roosevelt. When we come upon a page listing remedies for diarrhea in an infant, constipation, wind, and thrush, with only the notation "Mrs. Lee," we find it exciting to discover that this Mrs. Lee was the trained nurse who attended Mrs. Roosevelt at the birth of her only child. The remedies could mean just one thing, and Sara's concern with them pleases us not only for the glimpse it gives of a president-to-be in infancy, but also for its glimpse into the concerns of all mothers of that day.

This informative memento has been preserved because of two well-known facets of Mrs. Roosevelt's character. First, she never threw anything away; and second, she was thoroughly schooled in the Delano habit of writing everything down. Hardly a day passed by that she did not commit its happenings to paper. Hardly a delectable dish was served to her for which she did not request and usually note the recipe. For fifty-two years she preserved such items with firm energy and inflexible method. Inquiring minds of the future must be always in her debt because she did this.

The Household Book seems worth reproducing intact, if only as a guide to some domestic arts that are almost lost to us. Many of the old recipes will offer the modern cook a delightful challenge, and in printing them here we have tried to help out with translations into today's culinary vernacular. The transcript of the Household Book, with our notes, will be found at the end of this volume.

Our own real pleasure, however, has been in tracking down the clues to people and a way of life that are part of our recent past. Tantalized by the names, dates, and places which Sara Roosevelt included so meticulously, we found ourselves eager to identify them, and thus, willy-nilly, we were led back to the beginning—to the birth of the seventh child and fifth daughter to Warren Delano and his wife Catherine, in the middle of the nineteenth century.

II

The Delano Family of Algonac

THEY had wanted to call her Sarah Philippa—"Sarah" for her father's sister, and "Philippa" for Philippe De La Noye, the founder of the Delano family in America, who came to Plymouth in 1621.

It seemed a long and cumbersome name for a newborn baby, and her parents soon thought better of it and settled on just plain Sarah. It was a decision which pleased her seafaring grandfather Delano.

"Plane Sarah Delano is decidedly better—I think well of leaving out of her name Philippa," he wrote in September 1854 to his daughter Sarah Alvey Delano, for whom the baby was being named.

"Myself and wife are much pleased to hear that dear Katie and the sweet little one are doing so well and that all the other little ones are so happy and rejoicing in the gift and companionship of their little sister.

"We are having beautiful warm weather, and I learn from Warren that your grounds are putting on their natural garment of freshness and beauty. . . . My wife joins me in much love to you, Katie and all the dear ones, we hope to meet with you all on the Hudson in the course of the coming month."

Although it was September 21, the grounds of Algonac, the Delano home near Newburgh on the Hudson, were surprisingly fresh and beautiful after the summer heat. The latest Delano child was born into a smiling world: the September sun warm overhead, the Hudson rolling away past Mount Beacon and toward Storm King, a hazy blue at the foot of the still verdant highlands. The southern windows of Algonac framed this enchanting vista, and although the grounds lay at some distance from the river, it seemed as though the green lawns might almost reach into the water.

It was a wonderful place to be born, and a fine family to have been born into. For those who believe in such things, "plane Sarah," future mother of Franklin Delano Roosevelt, must have had a fairy godmother. Her father, Warren Delano II (son of Warren Delano I, the sea captain of Fairhaven, Massachusetts, he who delighted in plainness), was already, in 1854, a wealthy man. He had grown up in New Bedford in the glorious days of clipper ships and whalers. He had followed the sea, and then helped build the firm of Russell Sturgis & Co. in Hong Kong into one of the most powerful and successful Yankee tea export firms in the Orient.

With that energy and love of action characteristic of the Delanos, he had returned to Massachusetts, married Catherine Lyman of Northampton, in 1843, and immediately whisked his bride back to Hong Kong. A portrait painted by William Winter about the time of her marriage shows young Mrs. Delano as a dark-haired, dark-eyed young woman of considerable style and beauty, with a degree of firmness to her mouth, and a sweet expression. She was eighteen and her husband was thirty-three, side-whiskered, with an aquiline nose, clear candid eyes, and a warmth of manner and lack of pretense that made people feel "there could be nothing but pleasure in his society."

There is something almost breathless in the early history of this energetic couple. At a time when it took three to four months to reach the Orient, they traveled out and back within the space of three years; rented, then bought, a house in Lafayette Place, a stone's throw from where the Wanamaker store now stands in New York City; then moved up to Danskammer Point, above the city of Newburgh, for the summers, and began looking about for a suitable estate to purchase. Eventually Mr. Delano found a location which suited him, two miles north of Newburgh; and in 1851, eight years after his marriage, he bought some sixty-odd acres, beautifully wooded and planted to fruit trees, upon which a long, low house stood high above the river's bank.

Mr. Delano was by nature what his friend Andrew Jackson Downing, the great American landscape architect of Newburgh, called a "rural improver," and it was a matter of course that he should wish to make extensive alterations to both house and grounds. Mr. Downing, although extremely busy at that time in designing the arrangement of the grounds near the Capitol, the White House, and the Smithsonian Institution in Washington, at the invitation of President Fillmore, nevertheless found time to advise Mr. Delano upon the remodeling of "Algonac" and the laying out of gardens, walks, greenhouses, and so forth.

By 1852 the house had been altered and enlarged to include forty rooms; it had been painted the soft fawn color which Mr. Downing advised; and Mr. Delano had begun to enjoy that "accessible perfect seclusion" which, Mr. Downing declared, "is one of the most captivating features in the life of the country gentleman whose lot is cast on the banks of the Hudson—the broad Hudson which forms the grand feature in all these varied landscapes—the Hudson always so full of life in its numberless bright sails and steamers. One might fancy himself one thousand miles from all the crowded and busy haunts of men."

The rejuvenated "Algonac" was a towered and verandaed residence, with chambers of noble proportions. The entrance hall was nineteen feet square; from it the principal stairs went grandly up to the second floor. The drawing room at the left of the entrance measured more than eighteen by twenty-seven feet, with a bay that looked out over the sunset. There was a dining room; another parlor, sixteen by twenty feet; and the library, off which the break-fast room, later the schoolroom, opened—as well as a nine-teen-by-twenty-one-foot kitchen, a large laundry, a tub room, and a maze of pantries, washrooms, corridors, closets, and storerooms. Upstairs, the many bedrooms were equally com-modious.

The furnishings have been described as "palatial." Indeed, the beautiful Oriental objects of art which adorn Algonac today—the teakwood and porcelain screens, the mother-of-pearl inlaid bedstead, the round Chinese table in the central hall, the many pieces of carved jade, together with the Vic-torian carved brocade-upholstered suites selected by Mrs. Delano for her drawing room and parlor—give the impres-sion of a home of such taste and wealth as few American families in the eighteen-fifties could boast. It was a home where comfort and beauty were combined in a manner which even Mr. Downing would have considered ideal.

During the many uprootings which preceded Algonac the family had been growing at a true nineteenth-century pace. The first little daughter, born in China, had died soon after the Delanos returned to the United States. Another daughter, Louise, was born in 1846; a third daughter, Deb-orah (Dora), in 1847; and two years later Annie Lyman, the fourth daughter, arrived.

Before the move to Algonac, small Warren III had been born and died; and the year of the move there was a second son, also Warren III. Mr. Delano's unmarried brother Edward (Uncle Ned), and his sister Sarah, that "dear Auntie" for whom little Sara was named, had come to make their home at Algonac when they were not traveling; so that there was abundant affection and love waiting for the baby Sara (spelled without the "h" to distinguish her from the beloved aunt).

This dark-haired little girl—almost immediately nicknamed "Sallie"—must have had a delightful infancy. There was her nurse, Mary Bell, to care for her; there were Louise and Dora and Annie and Warren to play with, and Uncle Ned and Auntie and Mama, and above all Papa, to watch out for her and cherish her tenderly. There were golden days of sunlight in the gardens of Algonac, when the summer sun shone brightly, and clear silver days in winter, when the big sleigh was taken out and the whole family might cross the river on the ice to Beacon. There was plenty of everything, including gentleness and amiability among the grown-ups who surrounded her. This was a soil which should foster the growth of a happy and equable spirit.

For three years this idyllic existence continued, and the birth of a second son, this time Philippe, gave Sallie another playmate.

And then, in the fall of 1857, a great cloud of panic and depression appeared over the American horizon. On October 13, eighteen New York banks suspended payment to their depositors. The next day, all the banks in New York, with the exception of the Chemical, stopped specie payment, and the banks of other cities and states, from Maine to New Orleans and California, followed suit.

Warren Delano was among those wealthy men, pitied by the New York *Herald,* who, "occupying a high social position owing to their reputed wealth, have been suddenly precipitated from it by the crash which has engulfed so many noble fortunes and promising speculations. . . . What must be the misery of these people at being compelled to strip off their fine clothes, to lay aside their equipages and to quit their splendid mansions for some humble dwelling."

Mr. Delano, in addition to his profitable Oriental tea trade and his ships, which were the envy of the maritime world, had since his return from China acquired real-estate interests in New York City, as well as coal mines in eastern and western Pennsylvania, copper mines in Tennessee, and other mining interests. His fortune had been estimated at close to a million dollars, and he was generally thought of as one of the most successful businessmen of his day.

But the bitter wind of financial fright blew cold upon him, and while his wife and children were not stripped of their fine clothes, economies began to be practiced and a For Sale sign did certainly appear upon the gates of Algonac.

Yet who could afford to buy, let alone maintain, a country gentleman's estate with forty rooms, no matter how beautiful the view of the Hudson? After a battle against formidable odds, this shrewd, energetic, affable but hard-headed gentleman, at the age of fifty decided to start all over again. He left his wife and his six children—with another expected —in charge of Uncle Ned and Auntie, and sailed forth to build up a business in Hong Kong once more.

During his absence the household at Algonac continued to expand. Before the birth of Katherine (Kassie or Cassie) in 1860, while her Papa was halfway around the world, Mr. Delano's cousin, Nancy Church, came to make a long visit. This visit eventually lasted twenty-two years. "She made herself so important and so much loved, that she stayed with us always until she died. We called her Nannie," Sara Delano explained to her friend and biographer, Rita Halle Kleeman, author of *Gracious Lady*.

Nannie became Mrs. Delano's right-hand woman. She converted the breakfast room into a schoolroom and taught the children when they were little; she helped take care of them in all their minor illnesses; she fitted into the household at Algonac so admirably that "Cousin Katie" could not think of getting along without her.

At the end of two years Warren Delano, his fortunes still in a precarious state, but homesick for his family, chartered the square-rigged clipper ship *Surprise* (A. A. Low & Bros. owners), to bring them all out to Hong Kong. Mr. Abbot A. Low, of this same firm, leased Algonac for several years, since the attempt to sell had failed. The Delanos were once again on the move, after a record eleven years in one spot.

They all set sail in June 1862—Mama, the seven children, and Nannie; also an English nurse and a maid. What a wonderful adventure for small Sallie! Traveling to China to meet her Papa, and having a whole ship for her playground! One hundred and twenty days the voyage lasted —through the North and South Atlantic, around the Cape of Good Hope, up through the Indian Ocean and the Malay Archipelago. Twelve weeks out, on September 21, Sallie celebrated her eighth birthday, and the master of the *Surprise,* Captain Charles Ranlett, celebrated his twenty-eighth. So there were two birthday cakes baked in the galley, and roast goose, ham and vegetables, chicken dough, and pies for dinner. Mrs. Delano commented briefly, "Drank champagne. Captain hoisted the flags which looked prettily. . . . After tea all hands sang on deck." Of all Sallie's presents (carefully listed by Mama), she liked best the Shaker bonnet which dear Auntie had trimmed for her and sent along to be opened on her birthday. It was of light blue sarcenet silk, like a dress Sallie had once admired.

The next week the *Surprise* made Java Head. Sallie found this lively port "very beautiful, very tropical." All the children, with the exception of little Cassie, were allowed to go ashore, and they took with them their drawing books and crayons in order to make sketches of all the exciting and exotic birds and flowers. Their delineations of albatross were especially successful and were treasured in the family for years.

It was not until October 30 that the *Surprise,* after a hot and becalmed passage through the China Sea, sighted land once more. While they still seemed to be far out at sea, a small boat put out, and a tall slim gentleman, dressed all in white, steered her to the ship's side and sprang quickly up a ladder lowered for him. It was Warren Delano, come to embrace his family and take them to Rose Hill, the great house in Hong Kong which was to be their Chinese home.

A hemisphere away from Algonac, the children settled down, and Nannie took over their daily instruction once more—not in the breakfast room looking out upon the fair Hudson, but in a large schoolroom on the second floor of Rose Hill, with a view into gardens of palms and tree ferns and paths lined with pottery jars in which grew bright flowering plants. "Papa," as Sallie recalled, "had specially designed straight-backed chairs for us to sit in." Mr. Delano did not hold with children sitting slumped over their lessons.

Sallie studied French. She admitted to liking French very much. She also began to study music with her sister Dora, who was now sixteen and helped Nannie by teaching Sallie music one day and Warren the next.

"We had a little carriage"—brought in the *Surprise* from Algonac—"and ponies and various things to amuse us," Sallie's account continues. Their entertainment included band concerts, at which she thought the tunes quite solemn. "When we went to dine at the Chinese home of Papa's great Chinese friend, Mr. Howqua," she noted, "Papa told us children to pretend we liked Chinese food, though it was very strange to us." In later years she said this strange food had consisted of "every imaginable delicacy," and had been served on magnificent china and silver.

It can be only an assumption, but could her early acquaintance with the intricate seasoning and unaccustomed savor of Chinese fare have helped to influence the later culinary taste of a child who had hitherto been raised on a good American diet, consisting chiefly of meats and poultry and puddings and pies? It seems quite possible that her later predilection for curries made with garlic and green ginger, to be eaten with rice, as evidenced by the recipes in the Household Book, hint of a familiarity with an Oriental cuisine.

It is noteworthy that one of the mementos of this Oriental period is still to be seen in the house at Hyde Park: an enormous blue and white bowl in the library, which Dora brought home from Rose Hill. It is the sort of bathtub used in China in many foreign homes, and in this identical jar all the small Delanos once wriggled while Nannie or the nurse poured water over their shoulders.

There also clung to some remote corner of Sallie's mind the memory of the punkah, that large fan of muslin hung from the ceiling over the dining-room table and moved back and forth in warm weather by a rope pulled by a punkah coolie hidden behind a screen; of the unintelligible chatter of two Chinese tailors as they sat cross-legged, sewing for the household; of the joy and excitement of going to the races at the Happy Valley course and watching Warren, aged eleven, riding a small Arab horse to victory in the gentlemen's jockey race.

In spite of the fascinations of this foreign life, and the warmth of family atmosphere which Mama and Papa carried with them wherever they went, the first Christmas away from Uncle Ned and her "dearest sweetest Auntie" was a little difficult. There was no coasting down hills, a winter pastime of which she was passionately fond; there was no sleighing, there were no Christmas trees, nor the sharp clean smell of snow and ice in December, although Hong Kong seemed colder than she had expected. Sallie *did* wish she were with them all at home.

Her wish was shortly to come true, for after a year and a half at Rose Hill the Delanos reluctantly decided that the semitropical climate of Hong Kong was not good for the children. Furthermore, it was felt that it was time to supplement Nannie's admirable schoolroom with something more formal in the way of education, particularly for the two boys. So Warren, Sallie, and Philippe were given in charge of Annie, who at fifteen put her hair up "for the purpose of maintaining discipline," and these four were sent back to the United States under the care of Mr. P. S. Forbes of the firm of Russell & Company. With them went his son William. Young Mr. William Forbes was at this time engaged to Dora, and he must have found it somewhat trying to leave her and superintend her young sisters and brothers. However, with Annie's help, the long journey home by way of Saigon, Singapore, Aden, Suez, and France, with a hurried two weeks in Paris and London, was safely accomplished. Sallie's chief memory of this extended globe-trotting seems to have been a blue silk dress she got in Paris, with a low neck, long sleeves, and a guimpe of white muslin—a thoroughly feminine and natural reaction.

Uncle Ned and Auntie were waiting to receive their nephews and nieces with open arms, and to take them to the house which they then had on Eleventh Street in New York. Annie stayed there with them, Warren was sent to Colonel Miles' school at Brattleboro, Vermont, and the two little ones, Sallie and Phil, were sent to spend the winter in Northampton, with their mother's half-brother, Judge Samuel

Lyman—"where the climate did us much good," said Sallie, and they went to bed every evening at half-past seven.

By this time she had evinced a decided fondness for music, and so she took music lessons. She studied with a Mr. William Clark because Auntie thought she would get on better with a gentleman, and she found him very kind. She also studied "practical arithmetic as well as mental," and announced that she intended to make greater progress in French and get ahead of the others. She liked gymnastics because there she didn't have to wear crinoline. There is something about the set of the small determined mouth in the photographs taken just before she left China which would indicate that Miss Sara Delano at the age of ten had a mind of her own and a nice sense of her own capabilities.

This was, of course, at the time of the Civil War, and aside from her lessons Sallie engaged in a great deal of sewing for the soldiers. She made a soldier's shirt all by herself, and announced to Auntie and Annie that on rainy days she was going to knit "soldiers' stockings, and crocheting and those things, you know."

The child of ten and a half was to remember distinctly the April week in 1865 when all the houses in Northampton were lighted up and there were fireworks in honor of the Union's recent victories. She heard all the bells of the town ring and the cannon boom in celebration of Lee's surrender.

She noted that her father was very anxious to come home and enter the war, but could not leave China on account of his family. Also, he was by that time engaged in an enterprise directly tied up with the war effort, which not only started him once more on the road to financial betterment but was of direct aid to the North in the War between the States.

By means of his wide knowledge of the Chinese markets and his long-standing friendship with such important Chinese merchants as Mr. Howqua, he was able to ship opium home at a time when the Medical Bureau of the War Department was frantically in need of this most vital of medical supplies. There was nothing illegitimate about this business in any way, and indeed Warren Delano was known to Mr. Lincoln, and had held several semi-consular posts during his long stay in the Far East; but his opium negotiations were not very frequently spoken of by the family, probably because the very work had an unpleasant connotation. This story is told by Mr. Daniel Webster Delano in his book *Franklin Roosevelt and the Delano Influence.*

In any event, Mr. Delano's situation had so far improved that when he was called home in the summer of 1866, by the serious illness and subsequent death of his father, he saw no necessity for returning to Hong Kong. Algonac was still rented to the Lows. It would have been possible to stay on at Fairhaven, Massachusetts, in "The Homestead," which Captain Warren Delano had built in 1832, and which had undergone so many additions that it was quite capable of comfortably housing his son's large family, as well as Uncle Ned and Aunt Sarah. Next to Algonac, this house spelled home to the second Warren's children, for here they had come in relays every summer to visit their Grandpapa and his second wife. They knew the old village well, and were firm friends with the fishermen and sailors down at Grandpapa's wharf. They had played in the gardens and rummaged in the attic, and looked at all the pictures in the big books in the library, and filled themselves up to the brim from the cookie jar in the kitchen.

However, life in a small Massachusetts village did not offer the children the educational advantages which their Papa wished them to have, and so it was decided to spend the time in Europe until they could once more come to rest upon the banks of the Hudson.

Sallie's previous determination to get ahead of the others in French stood her in good stead, for the first year of this educational exile was spent in an apartment in Paris in the rue de Presbourg, and it was here she celebrated her twelfth birthday.

She described the festivities in a letter to "My darling Uncle Ned" as follows: "The day before yesterday was my birthday and I was twelve years old. I got a great many presents. I will tell you what they were. Mama gave me a lovely little work-basket, which I was very much pleased with. Nannie gave me a very nice book called 'Famous girls who have become good and illustrious women.' I wanted a book very much. Dora gave me a very nice sun umbrella which will do for sun or for rain it is just as nice as it can be and is made of brown silk. On my birthday Maggie, May and Arthur Carey spent the afternoon with me and I had a very nice birthday party. We played tableaux all about a rich Italian family and we were dressed very handsomely and had a great many scenes. . . ."

How comforting for a little girl to be able to have her dearest friend to a birthday party so far away from home! Maggie Carey's mother, whom Sallie called aunt, was a sister of the Aunt Laura (Astor) who had married Papa's brother, Franklin Delano; so the two families were intimate, and the two little girls, Sallie and Maggie, spent several years in the same European schools, carrying with them, no doubt, a faint flavor of American independence and well-born assurance.

In Paris, Dora was married to Will Forbes, and Sallie and Cassie attended their first wedding, dressed alike in silvery gray poplin. After the wedding the Delanos went to a German resort called Connstadt, where Sallie might take a cure. For she had developed rheumatic fever in the spring of 1867, when the Forbeses had left for Hong Kong, and she had been quite ill. Youth, a naturally strong constitution, and perhaps the sulphur baths, presently restored her to health and she accompanied Mama and Papa and the others to Dresden, where she met her friend Maggie again. The Delano and Carey girls attended school and learned to speak German flawlessly. Sallie noted that "some of us studied German and music." They were all taken to the art galleries, as well as to many operas and concerts, and given all the advantages of such a rich cultural center as Dresden had become in the middle of the nineteenth century.

In the spring the family divided. Mama and Papa took the younger children and Louise back to Algonac, from which they had been gone so long. Annie, Warren, and Sallie stayed in Germany, to polish off their education, under the care of Uncle Ned and Auntie, who apparently liked nothing better than to be in charge of nephews and nieces. Annie and Warren attended school at Hanover, and Sallie went to live in the family of the Burgomaster's daughter at Celle. There she became a pupil in a German *Töchterschule*— freely translated: school for young ladies—and soon fell into the strict German way of doing things: school from eight to twelve and from two to four, music lessons at four o'clock, right after school, twice a week. After three months she had made such progress that she noted she was shortly to have all her lessons with the German girls. Her associates were not all German, however. Another young friend from America, Nelly Blodgett, whose father, Mr. William Tilden Blodgett, owned an estate in Beacon, had come to Germany to be polished too. Although she did not attend Sallie's *Töchterschule,* she was close enough to Hanover to join the Delanos from time to time, and a friendship was cemented which lasted for a lifetime. Her admonition, just before the Delanos sailed for home, to "think often of your loving friends," found Sallie affectionately ready to obey.

Benevolent Uncle Ned and Auntie made their headquarters in Hanover, so that the children had someone close at hand to turn to, someone to take them on delightful vacation trips—to the Island of Ruegen one year and to the Harz Mountains the next.

Uncle Ned and Auntie must have been exuberant traveling companions, full of gaiety and adventure. Uncle Ned, in particular, appears to have been a great jokester. But if he furnished the humor, Auntie was relied upon for equally solid comfort. "Could you enclose a thaler in your next letter?" queried Sallie from school. "I keep an account of what I spend."

The years of travel, between 1862 and 1870, during which Sallie was absent from Algonac, assuredly laid the foundation for a thorough linguistic education in French and German, an appreciation of the classical arts, a catholic taste and versatile performance in music, and a more than superficial understanding of European culture. It was the kind of education suitable for a gentleman's daughter, for a young woman of more than average mental ability, who did not wish to become merely another china-painting, silk-embroidery and pretty-sentiment kind of young miss, such as were being turned out by droves in the finishing schools of America at this time.

It is a testimonial to their Papa's breadth of vision and understanding of the world that he gave his daughters a preparation for mature life which made them secure in their accomplishments, which enabled them to comprehend the minds and tongues of people of other nations, and which assisted them all to such savoir faire, assurance, and practical knowledge as few young ladies had at their command eighty years ago. It is further remarkable that the long years away from home did not leave Sallie rootless. The large family at home, the incessant letters, the feeling of being loved and missed in the family circle, wherever Papa and Mama and Cousin Nannie and the others might be—this bound the child tightly to her American heritage and left her what she had been from birth—a sprig of Yankee stock transplanted to the Hudson and firmly attached to the valley of her birth.

To this valley she returned in July of 1870. Not that she —or her parents—considered her education to be finished, but that two circumstances made it desirable to have Sallie back at Algonac. Her oldest sister, Louise, had died in 1869, after a long and lingering illness, apparently contracted during the days in China. Papa grieved deeply over this loss, and now wanted all his children about him. Also, the menacing clouds of the Franco-Prussian War had begun rolling up over the horizon. Auntie, Annie, Warren, Sallie, and Cousin Fred Hitch (to whom Annie later became engaged), with two servant women, managed to get passage on the *Westphalia,* the last German steamer to leave before war was declared.

After eight years abroad, Sallie was at home again. Papa met them all at the dock at Hoboken and, by dint of good management and considerable effort, got them and their thirty-three packages loaded on the train reaching Algonac before seven o'clock. Mr. Delano was a pious man and moved by simple, living faith. He earnestly and sincerely thanked God for His loving-kindness in bringing the family together again in health and peace, with aspirations and hopes for future usefulness and happiness.

Now began a family life at Algonac peculiar to the setting and the time, rich in association with family, friends, and relatives; bound together by Papa's sense of energy, discipline, and order; mellowed by Mama's serene and loving ways. Since the birth of Cassie in 1860 there had been two more children added to the Delano quiver: Frederic Adrian, born in China in 1863; and lovely little Laura, born in 1864.

There were grownups, young ladies, and little boys and girls and babies and horses and pigs and cows at Algonac. There were a cook and a cook's maid—important members of the staff, for there were rarely less than twelve or fourteen at table—a gardener, his helper, a coachman, the mother's helper, Elise, brought over from Germany, and Nannie, still teaching abc's in the old breakfast room.

Sallie, not quite sixteen, tall, with great elegance of bone and bearing, and with the refinement of a foreign education in her manner, found that she knew the German language as well as her own and that she was better versed in German literature than in English; so she returned to her studies and continued with her music lessons and drawing. This left her half in the schoolroom and half out of it. Since by sixteen the Delano girls were expected to help their mother entertain, she made the adjustment, it would seem, by dint of bearing down rather haughtily on the young ones and permitting no liberties.

Except under unusual circumstances—as when, for example, upon Christmas Day the Irish cook, Bridget, announced that she was going to spend the day in church and would not be able to cook the Christmas dinner—apparently Sallie took very little part in the work of the household, large as it was, and thus was able to concentrate on her piano lessons and drawing.

Papa kept a very firm hand upon the administration of the entire estate—from working like a Trojan, superintending the men who were cutting down trees, to laying oilcloth in the back hall, to hiring servants (both inside and out). Mama took care of the marketing, and one gets the impression that she rather enjoyed attending to the smaller details of housekeeping. She frequently drove to Newburgh, then a pretty village with a long and very wide main street running down to the river. Here she bought eggs and coffee and vinegar and listened to "little pieces of Gossip."

It was naturally she who kept an eye on the date when the babies could leave off their flannel drawers; but it was her husband who agreed to pay Mary Humphrey, the new cook, eighteen dollars a month, on her assurance that she was a "first-rate cook, clean, economical, good-tempered, a good bread and cake maker." Mary certainly deceived her employer, for eight months later Mr. Delano found her "drunk as a pig," and packed her off to Newburgh in the wagon.

This man of energy trained rosebushes, sawed wood, put down twenty-three chickens and five turkeys in the ice in the icehouse just for an experiment, kept a constant lookout for new horses for his stable, and altogether reigned like a benevolent but absolute monarch.

Sister Annie, the oldest of the Delano daughters living at home, was the mainstay of the household. (This she seems to have been all her life, with the exception of the few years of her marriage which she spent in Hong Kong.) And she was apparently the sister who took most interest in household affairs. It will be noticed that ten of the recipes in the Household Book come from A. L. D. H.

When candy-pulls were in progress in the Algonac kitchen, or if there were some new dainty to try, it was Annie who led the culinary endeavors and surprised Papa by her successes with molasses candy and apple charlotte.

It was Annie and Sallie who played the piano to entertain their parents' dinner guests—although one wonders how the guests could have stayed awake to appreciate the music after a dinner of oysters, soup, bass, mutton chops, roast turkey, birds, and tipsy cake, with which were served claret, sherry, and champagne!

"Life was very regular at Algonac," was Sallie's comment to Mrs. Kleeman on this period of her life. "Friends

visited us; no large house parties, just relatives and friends
who came one or two or three at a time."

The family was very regular in its attendance at the Unitarian church, and Papa was careful to note the text of the
sermon and his opinions upon the minister's discourse,
usually favorable. Mama was also a faithful churchgoer, but
her thoughts about the sermon might sometimes have been
led astray by the fact that she was wearing a new purple silk
with a polonaise of black grenadine.

"There were always saddle horses, so with riding and
driving and friends coming and going, life was quite full,"
Sallie continued. It apparently took Sallie a short time to get
accustomed to riding again. Annie noted that the first time
Sallie rode Dollie the mare, the horse buck-jumped and
rather frightened her. Annie herself, always a fine horse-
woman, rode Dollie a week later and found her "quite good
under saddle, her trot pretty easy, but mouth hard."

The little mare cannot be positively identified, but perhaps it is upon her that Sallie is mounted sidesaddle in a
snapshot taken in November 1873. Those were the days
when young ladies wore dark riding habits with long full
skirts, tight little jackets, and fetching hats with soft white
feathers folded up against the crown. No wonder the neighbors stared behind parted curtains when the handsome Delano girls rode by.

There were, of course, parties and picnics, too—fifty to a
dance at Algonac, which all pronounced a success, and for
which, Mama could report, the oysters were good; Fourth
of July picnic celebrations, during which tar-barrels were
burned for illumination in the evening; invitations to Sallie
for Commencement at Princeton, and invitations to West
Point; croquet parties on the lawn; "all hands" to the
Gordons for a dance, at which "scolloped" oysters and ducks
were the fare. There was sleighing on the river and coasting

on the hills in the winter, with hot chocolate afterward. There were delightful boat rides in the summer, and, best of all, there was always congenial companionship for Sallie, not only with her contemporaries but particularly with her Papa, with whom she had a close bond of affection and understanding.

Busy as he was with the mining and real-estate interests which again engrossed him, taking him to New York at least twice a week, Warren Delano was never too much occupied to see that Sallie got to the city for her singing lessons, or to participate in a lively fashion in all the affairs and concerns of his children.

He shuttled back and forth across the Hudson constantly, either to bring Laura home from school in Fishkill or to take her back after a week end at home; he worried about the health of Philippe, who showed alarming signs of the same debilitating illness which had taken Louise from them; he gave some thought to the discipline of young Fred; and he naturally assisted Warren III, who had been graduated from Harvard Scientific School in 1874, to make a suitable connection with the Union Mining Company. Papa and Mama and Annie and Sallie went down to Baltimore for Warren's wedding to Miss Jennie Walters of that city in 1876. This event caused the family much pleasure, for Warren had been engaged since his college days, and Miss Jennie, his bride, was a young lady of marked intellectual attainments and some sound ideas about homemaking, too, as her entries in the Household Book, signed J. W. D., can testify.

Papa seems to have taken a most wise course about his children's love affairs. He looked over his daughters' beaux and teased the girls about the avalanche of young men who came to call in the evening. He was not perturbed when he observed noticeable symptoms of one or several of them falling in love with one or several of his girls, but he did gently and firmly indicate those suitors of whom he could not approve.

On those occasions when there were no suitors or other callers, and the weather was too bad for outdoor pleasure, there would be a little card-playing—whist—and music to make the evening pass quietly and agreeably. According to Sallie, "There was always reading aloud and many wonderful books gave us all pleasure. It seems to me now that most of the standard literature that I read in my young days came to me in that delightful and easy way and we took turns in reading while others worked." The novels of Mr. Dickens, Mr. Thackeray, Sir Walter Scott, Henry James, Jane Austen, and Charles Kingsley were all read aloud in the bay-windowed drawing room at Algonac, with Annie and Nannie, Auntie and Mama and Sallie painting or embroidering or knitting, while one read and the others listened, snug before the fire on cold or rainy days.

At eighteen, although there was no formal debut, Sallie was considered out in society. She spent several months each winter with Maggie Carey or Nelly Blodgett, and the young ladies were permitted to attend balls, driven in a carriage and chaperoned by a maid. Kittie Crummie, the sewing woman who had come to Algonac every spring and fall for many years to "do" for the family, was considered not to have quite the smartest touch for Sallie's first ball gowns. Therefore Sallie was allowed to go to her Mama's dressmaker in New York for three delightful concoctions—one of pink, one of blue, and one of white, all made exactly alike, with tulle skirts and trains, and small pointed satin waists with tiny sleeves. Beneath this loveliness she wore taffeta petticoats with lace flounces, which she pinned to her outer skirt with safety pins, so that they would billow out around her when she danced. Sallie at eighteen, a cloud of pink tulle floating about her, her dark hair drawn smoothly back from her forehead, with just a hint of a beau-catcher curling around her temples, must indeed have made many a young man's heart beat more swiftly.

During this period of social gaiety, Maggie Carey was married to M. Alphonse De Stuers, Chargé d'Affaires for the Netherlands. "The nicest *foreigner* I have ever met," Sallie confided to her parents. She was, of course, asked to be a bridesmaid at the wedding, which took place in the Carey house on Madison Avenue and Thirty-fourth Street, and she wore a gauze frock of deep red tulle, which must have suited her to perfection. It is noteworthy that the other brides-maids also bore historic New York names: Emily Astor, Daisy Rutherford, and Minnie Rhinelander.

The Delanos belonged in what was considered the best society in New York. Among these were friends of many years' standing, such as the senior Theodore Roosevelts, whose daughter Anna ("Bammie") was one of Sallie's girl-hood intimates; and the William Astors. Actually, since Papa's brother, Franklin Delano, had married Mr. Astor's sister Laura, the Delanos and the Astors considered them-selves part of the same family circle. Uncle Frank and Aunt Laura lived in a beautiful house called Steen Valetje, in Barrytown, about twenty miles above Hyde Park on the Hudson, and since they were childless, Warren's children be-came almost as close to them as if they had been their own. The Franklin Delanos frequently came to Algonac, and no spring and summer ever went by that Annie and Sallie and Cassie did not ferry across the river to Beacon and take the train up-river to spend a week or ten days at a time with this kind and generous aunt and uncle.

So it was a matter of course that Sallie attended one of Mrs. William Astor's famous evening parties. *The* Mrs. Astor had already set out in the early seventies to capture command of

New York society. She initiated a lavishness in entertaining by comparison with which the simple sleigh rides and hot chocolate at Algonac, or the fifty guests on the gala evening when Mama thought the oysters were good, were childishly simple pastimes. "Society," remarked the New York *Herald,* "is never quite satisfied with itself until it has danced at least once in the season at Mrs. Astor's."

The floral decorations for this event were positively overwhelming: a profusion of roses, spring flowers, orange trees in full fruit, orchids in every nook and corner. The great Dresden china vases were filled with jonquils, lilies of the valley, lilacs, and roses, with pink and white azaleas at the base. The little reception room was devoted to American Beauty roses, and the drawing rooms were filled with roses of many varieties and annunciation lilies. In the midst of this hot-house prodigality, Mrs. Astor stood alone in the middle drawing room, receiving her guests, a rivière of solitaires about her neck, a great diamond stomacher over the appropriate spot, a tiara on her head—in later days on her black wig. The cotillion favors were also astonishing: trumpets, castanets, long wands fringed with gold and silver tinsel, ribbons, bells, lace fans, and lace hats. What a collection for a young lady to hang upon her mirror!

The supper, served by Pinard, was rich beyond all digesting; and the guests in this setting of ostentation and elegance noted that Mr. Astor, purveyor of such costliness, was rarely present to greet them.

By contrast, Papa and Mama never did anything for show only, and never led people to make false assumptions. They made their girls feel secure and happy. They gave them the luxuries which were considered in good taste, and a thorough acquaintance with the best in the world of art, literature, and music. With such a background, a ball at Mrs. Astor's, a reception and ball for the Grand Duke Alexei of

Russia, the first performance of *Lohengrin,* with Christine Nilsson, were diversions which could be eagerly enjoyed but did not overawe. This, as fate arranged matters, was an eclectic schooling for a lifetime of social contact with royalty, nobility, on down through the lesser ranks of plain American aristocracy.

After six years of life at home, during which she grew up from an almost finished schoolgirl to an accomplished and beautiful young lady, Sallie made preparations to go abroad again. It seemed an opportunity too good to miss, as Dora and Will Forbes, who had been home on a visit, were going back to China by way of Europe and would take this younger sister with them. They sailed, in the fall of 1876, to England, which Sallie did not know as thoroughly as the Continent, and where she indulged in a thrilling revel of sightseeing and music. The newly married De Stuers had been transferred to London, so she had the pleasure of being with her dear Maggie and being guided about by Maggie's husband, that "nice foreigner." Sallie, with a rare touch of humor, confessed to keeping up the reputation of the Delano family for hearty eating, and found that the London air made her appetite something fearful.

While in London she also did some shopping, but tried to be careful about what she bought, planning ahead as to what would be most useful at home, so that if she acquired a new waterproof, the old one could be given to one of her sisters. This she called "taking thought for the morrow," and it was a characteristic way of thinking which deserves emphasis.

In January 1877, after a short visit in Paris with Dora's in-laws, the Forbeses and Sallie sailed on the *Anadie* for Hong Kong. Sallie found Hong Kong harbor "too lovely," and more beautiful than she remembered it to be. But her enjoyment of the races, the balls, the visits, and the shopping tours which Dora had promised her was cut short by the decision to sail for Europe again only a month after her arrival. In 1877 a young lady of twenty-two did not travel from Hong Kong to New York by herself, and the fact that a Mr. and Mrs. Pomeroy were willing to chaperon her back to Europe snatched Sallie away from Rose Hill when she had scarcely had time to get reacquainted with the round porcelain bathtubs and the punkahs. She returned on the same steamer on which she had gone out, in company with the Pomeroys and her sister Annie's fiancé, Fred Hitch. This was a little disappointing, for she and Papa had planned that she should come home by way of California, thus completing a world tour. However, as she pointed out, she could not wait indefinitely for somebody to chaperon her to San Francisco, particularly as Annie and Fred Hitch were planning to be married in the fall, and Sallie was, of course, to be a bridesmaid.

She arrived in Europe at the end of April, spent two months in Paris and London, buying clothes, getting presents for Annie, going to the opera (for which she had developed a fondness that lasted throughout her life), and then, still under Mrs. Pomeroy's wing, sailed for Algonac, which was becoming every day more lovely and for which she yearned, if not with homesickness, with impatience and longing.

Annie and Fred Hitch were married in the fall. The West Point band played music from *Lohengrin,* and Sallie and Cassie were bridesmaids.

Our "Sallie" had now become "Miss Delano"—"the beautiful Miss Delano," people usually added.

Annie's place as pillar of the household and Mama's mainstay was empty. For several years, Sallie seems not to have had the interest in the kitchen that Annie had always shown, and there appear to have been no apple charlottes or other dainties prepared as surprises for Papa.

Instead, Miss Delano was busy attending assembly balls, going to the opera in New York with Papa, enjoying performances of *Pinafore* in Newburgh, taking music lessons of Mr. Wadsworth, and dancing at West Point hops.

In the winter of 1879 her beloved Auntie became seriously ill in Rome, New York, and Sallie and Papa went to her at once. Their arrival was a great comfort to poor Alvey—as Papa frequently called his sister. Sallie and Auntie and Harriet Wood, her aunt's companion, were eventually brought down to Fishkill, and the invalid was conveyed over the river in the small bobsleigh fitted with a long rattan chair and plenty of fur robes, with four or five men to push her across the ice. Poor Alvey had a long siege of it, not leaving the house until May. However, she was well enough later in the summer to go back to Fairhaven, where Sallie and her youngest sister, Laura, then on vacation from Miss Wagner's school in Fishkill, joined her for six weeks in their grandfather's rambling old house.

It was during this visit that Auntie gave her dear niece and namesake a small blank-paged book, approximately eight inches long and six inches wide, on the title page of which Auntie wrote, "Sara Delano from S. A. D. Fair Haven, 29 Aug. '79."

Scrapbooks had become very fashionable by then—books in which young ladies pasted recipes, bits of poetry, short stories, or other odds and ends from magazines and daily papers; or in which they wrote their thoughts, or got their friends to write autographs and sentiments. Sallie must have intended this for a recipe book at once, for the first entry is "H. W.'s receipt for *Orange Marmalade,*" dated very shortly after Auntie had given Sallie her present. Harriet Wood also contributed a recipe for meringues before Sallie went home.

Two recipes from Annie, now living in Shanghai, were entered before Sallie left Fairhaven, and on her arrival at Algonac she presumably copied in the recipe for Mrs. Johnston's Laplanders, which she had acquired on a visit to Plainfield several months before.

Now it would seem that Miss Delano, in spite of the round of social activity which occupied her days, was perhaps beginning to take a heartier interest in the management of a home than she had shown in the past. A natural question would be: had thoughts of a home of her own turned her attention to housekeeping matters? No written evidence has been found to suggest that this was so. Mr. H. J. Ramsdell, always a frequent caller at Algonac, continued to drop in for tea, or to plan parties to his Salisbury paper mills, only a short drive from Newburgh. Mr. Charles A. Robbins (who later married Kassie) called and asked for the young ladies. Miss Delano took a party of fourteen to Lake Mohonk in four carriages; the young people had a pleasant trip and returned the next day. Miss Bammie Roosevelt, sister of Theodore, Jr., and her brother Elliott, came up for a few days and joined an excursion party to West Point.

Then Papa got lumbago, and during his incapacitating illness it was Sallie who paid the laborers for him and, everybody else being busy, managed to get the house in rather good order. Auntie had returned from Fairhaven, her health no better, and although Dr. Smith Ely, the family physician in Newburgh, had diagnosed part of her trouble as a "floating sinew in her right knee," she suffered greatly and was more or less of an invalid through the fall and winter.

Just five days after New Year's 1880, the unobtrusive always faithful Nannie began to complain of shortness of breath, and within three days there was another invalid in the household to be cared for. Dr. Ely reported that Nannie had a serious affliction of one side of the heart, complicated by a kidney disease, and matters looked very grave. It was only two days before her death that he prescribed the broth, the recipe for which Sallie entered in her book.

Nannie died during the night of January 18, watched over, until they saw the end approaching, by two helpful servants in this house of illness—Jane, a maid, and Rosa, the cook. Rosa had been a member of the household for seven years and seemed almost like one of the family in this time of crisis. (She must have given Sallie her puff recipe just about the time of Nannie's fatal illness.)

Grief had not come so poignantly to Algonac since the death of sister Louise, eleven years before. Nannie, their dear friend and cousin, with whom they had spent such full and happy years, and who had mothered and taught each Delano baby in turn, was gone, and Papa felt that her death was a blow that more than killed.

Mama and Papa took her back to Fairhaven to be buried, leaving Sallie in charge of the household and of Auntie, who was by this time far too ill to travel. The house seemed very lonely with Mama and Papa and Nannie gone, but Sallie and Kassie brought Harriet Wood downstairs and made her sit with them while *Guy Mannering* was read aloud.

Harriet now slipped into the niche of companion and housekeeper at Algonac, in an unofficial kind of way. She had been with Auntie for at least ten years, and through the bad winter of 1879–80 must have been of immeasurable help to Mama and Sallie. Her recipes for beef tea and calf's head stem from this period when an invalid's diet had to be prepared.

Auntie continued ailing all through the spring, but her condition was not such as to cause any grave alarm, and the family routine went on much as before. Papa still made trips to New York at least twice a week, and Mr. Ramsdell continued to call. Miss Delano now began taking an active part in the question of household personnel, and, when the waitress and the kitchen maid left, engaged two others in New York. Her social schedule was still as stimulating as before, and the attractive Miss Delano at twenty-five was a guest much sought after in the circle of her New York friends. Upon a certain evening in this spring of 1880 she was asked to the Madison Avenue home of Mrs. Theodore Roosevelt, Sr., now a widow, one of the most charming hostesses in New York. The other guests included a Mr. Crowninshield of Boston, Miss Bammie Roosevelt, Miss Corinne Roosevelt—a younger sister—and a Mr. James Roosevelt of Hyde Park, New York—a widower. This Mr. Roosevelt was a cousin of the Theodore Roosevelts, and a business acquaintance whom Sallie had heard her papa mention many times.

Mr. Roosevelt looked at Miss Delano and saw a tall young woman with dark eyes and dark hair piled in puffs on top of her head, wide dark brows accentuating the harmony of her features. Miss Delano, looking at Mr. Roosevelt, saw a slender and urbane gentleman of medium height, past fifty, whose hazel eyes had a quizzical expression and whose dark side-whiskers, beginning to be flecked with gray, must of necessity have reminded her somewhat of her papa.

Their hostess claimed that Mr. Roosevelt never took his eyes off her charming feminine guest, and talked to her all the time.

There can be no conclusive evidence about this. But it can be positively stated that on May 7, 1880, Papa took Sallie to Fishkill, and she then continued on to Hyde Park with the Roosevelts (Mrs. Theodore Roosevelt, Bammie, and Corinne). Sallie stayed for a week—a very important week.

Fifty-two years later, on May 8, 1932, she wrote to her son from Hyde Park: "Just 51 years yesterday I came to visit. . . . If I had not come then, I should now be 'old Miss Delano' after a rather sad life! . . . I said 51 years, it is really 52 years since I came to visit in May."

III

The Roosevelt Family of Hyde Park

A LITTLE more than two miles north of Poughkeepsie, Dutchess County, New York, the traveler hurrying
to Albany over the Albany Post Road may notice on his left
two gateposts built of blocks of gray stone. They are old and
weathered and do not stand quite straight. The drive which
leads between them and up to a large yellow house is lined
with ancient trees. This is Rosedale, in the town of Hyde
Park, the home to which Isaac Roosevelt, M. D., moved early
in the nineteenth century and in which his granddaughter,
Miss Ellen Roosevelt, still lives.

The doctor, fifth in direct descent from the Claes Marten-
zen van Rosenvelt who established the Roosevelt family in
New Amsterdam in the seventeenth century, had lately become a family man, the father of a son, James, named for his
grandfather James. The latter lived in Mount Hope, a roomy
square house standing high on the hill almost directly across
the road from Rosedale, but over the line in the town of
Poughkeepsie.

It has been stated that Dr. Isaac's offspring was born in
Hyde Park on July 16, 1828, but since his parents did not
leave Mount Hope until 1832 or thereabouts, it is more
than likely that their first-born actually came into the world,
to the delight of all his connections, in one of the high-

ceilinged bedchambers of his paternal grandfather's country home.

The Roosevelts were solid people. They were keen at business—all but Isaac—and at the same time fond of good horseflesh and everything that went on out-of-doors. With an unusual affinity for the soil and country life, they managed to combine shrewd business acumen and banking proficiency.

The grandfather of the Rosedale Isaac, also named Isaac, was the only member of the family who had actively taken part in politics or government. His contributions toward the success of the American Revolution were so outstanding that he had been nicknamed "the Patriot."

The Patriot's son James inherited his father's profitable sugar refinery in New York and was for many years associated with the Bank of New York. In 1819 he moved to Dutchess County and built up Mount Hope, to which he retired as frequently as possible, for he liked farming and wanted to spend his old age on the green slopes above the Hudson and raise horses. He and his third wife, Harriet Howland, were substantial, kindly, white-haired, and rosy-cheeked when young James knew them—full of comfort, often of a financial sort.

How such a well-planted and hard-headed business man as this Mr. James Roosevelt managed (by his first wife, Maria Walton) to have a son like Dr. Isaac is one of the mysteries which heredity cannot always explain. The son was the antithesis of the father and the grandfather. He despised politics and hated business. Having graduated from Princeton with the class of 1808, he then attended the College of Physicians and Surgeons at Columbia University and was admitted to the practice of medicine. A strange education for a man who could not bear the sight of blood, nor bring himself to look upon the suffering of any living thing!

In 1820 Isaac no longer pretended to be a professional man, and returned to his father's house at Mount Hope to live. Here he spent his time puttering about the gardens, tending livestock, and, until he was thirty-seven, leading the life of a reclusive bachelor, taking great care of his health and interesting himself in the affairs of the old Dutch Reformed Church in Poughkeepsie. In 1827, if not to the astonishment of his friends and relatives, certainly to the surprise of twentieth-century biographers, Isaac married Miss Mary Rebecca Aspinwall.

His choice of Miss Aspinwall as a bride was a happy one, for she was a vigorous and amiable young woman and made Dr. Isaac a loving and gentle wife; but it added a further knot to the genealogical puzzle of Roosevelt intermarriages, which almost defy clear explanation. Isaac was the stepson of Miss Aspinwall's aunt. Their son James, therefore, was his grandfather's grandnephew by marriage.

Despite this complicated heredity, the baby throve, flourished, and was baptized on December 2, 1828, in the Dutch Reformed Church at Poughkeepsie, by the Reverend Mr. Cornelius Cuyler. This clergyman, a graduate of Union College, class of 1806, was well known to the Roosevelts, made frequent calls at Rosedale, and so it is possible that it was his advice which was followed on a matter of some importance to James eighteen years later.

Now that he was the head of a family, it was natural that Dr. Isaac should wish to establish his own home. He set about acquiring land across the Post Road and north from his father's property, and prepared a solid gabled house, plain and ample. From his grounds he could look across to the village of Highland and those palisade-like rocks upon which the competing oarsmen of later generations painted the initials of their universities at Poughkeepsie Regatta time. The prospect was placid. It lacked that grandeur which frames the Hudson River banks farther to the south, but perhaps this suited the Isaac Roosevelts better.

In about 1832 Dr. and Mrs. Isaac Roosevelt were able to move from Mount Hope to Rosedale. Although it stood closer to the river than Algonac, this house had none of the wide sweep and long view of the Hudson, nor that skillful blending of shadow and sunlight on the grounds which Mr. Downing's skill and Mr. Delano's taste had produced near Newburgh.

Rosedale stood darkly in trees, with wide verandas somberly shaded. The rooms were large and uncramped, but without that Oriental wealth of decoration which flooded the Algonac rooms with color and warmth. Dr. Isaac Roosevelt had fine mahogany furniture in his home, oil paintings heavily framed in gold, silver services and crystal, and a drawing room from which one could see the sunset on the water; but because of the retired life he led, with a family consisting only of Mrs. Roosevelt and their small son James, and no great commotion of children and nurses to upset the household routine, it was a quiet place, quietly furnished, quietly lived in.

Dr. Isaac, owning considerable land adjacent to his residence, now devoted himself almost entirely to the management of his farm, tending to the haying, planting more melons and grapes, buying oxen, reading, studying, and shrinking further and further from violent contact with life.

There is scant record of small James' earliest years. When the boy was nine years old, not wishing to have him go away from home, his parents entered him in the Poughkeepsie Collegiate School, newly founded by Mr. Charles Bartlett, A. M., and conducted "on philosophical principles."

Building in imitation of the Parthenon, Mr. Bartlett had erected an elegant pseudo-Greek-temple school on the top of one of the highest hills in the vicinity of the "flourishing and beautiful village of Poughkeepsie," and had set out to educate masculine youth in a manner novel to many schoolboys of the period. He announced that reference was invariably to be had "to the nature of the juvenile mind and constant efforts employed to develope [sic] its powers in their natural order and to preserve them in their relative strength . . . ," and that while the strictest order was enjoined, "such discipline would be employed as would most effectively tend to call into action the moral sense of the scholar."

The curriculum consisted of orthography, reading, writing, English grammar, geography, rhetoric, logic, mathematics, history, natural philosophy, political economy, civil polity, the French and Spanish languages, and for those who intended going to college—of whom young James Roosevelt was one—Latin and Greek.

This would seem like a heavy scholastic load for a small boy to carry, to say nothing of the smothering overemphasis upon "moral sense." But one hundred and twenty years ago a boys' school which paid more attention to "the nature of the juvenile mind" then to a birch cane, and which punished "irregular conduct" chiefly by "disapprobation of the instructors and private and public censure," was refreshingly lenient and progressive.

There can be no doubt that Mr. Bartlett trained his pupils well. For some years the Poughkeepsie Collegiate School continued to educate the sons of the well-to-do families up and down the Hudson River, and not the least consideration in sending a boy there was the fact that he would associate with "gentlemen's sons."

In 1840, when James was twelve, a second son was born

to his parents—John Aspinwall Roosevelt, who naturally became Johnny. It is extraordinary that James was apparently always called by his full name, and that he was distinguished from his grandfather James only by the appellation Junior. He was not, somehow, the sort of boy or man who looked to his contemporaries like "Jim."

By the time the boy was fourteen, he had been sent to school to a Mr. Alexander Hyde in Lee, Massachusetts, where he continued to work at Greek and Latin, preparatory to entering college. His grandfather, having undertaken to pay for his schooling, was naturally pleased to hear that he was doing well with Mr. Hyde, and his father expressed himself as gratified that James was prosecuting his studies with application and diligence, but characteristically was worried lest his constitution should in the least degree be injured by study.

This paternal solicitude for his son's health would appear to have been wholly needless, for James was a strong, well-grown youth, who seems not to have had more than minor illnesses in his life, and to have been in no danger of turning into an unwholesome bookworm. He had inherited his grandfather's love of the out-of-doors and of good horses, and was, even in his teens, exceptionally self-reliant and reliable, with a warmth of personality and humor which made him almost universally referred to from his earliest days as "dear James."

The question of his higher education appears to have been a matter of extensive discussion and debate in family circles, and after a good deal of indecision James was finally registered at New York University in 1844. He was to live at his Roosevelt grandparents' home on Bleecker Street, in order not to be cast too wildly into the distractions of city life. The Roosevelt home was not far from the house on the same street in which his Aspinwall grandparents lived. Here his jolly Grandmother Aspinwall had cross-stitch covers on her nice old mahogany furniture and baked her famous crullers. But even such an intimate family arrangement as this drew forth criticism from his mother's uncle, who opined that if James were permitted to attend New York University he would become a dandy and would walk Broadway with his cane.

These dire predictions never came to pass, for during the short time he was at the University James distinguished himself and enjoyed life without falling prey to the hazards with which loving and solicitous relatives imagined him to be surrounded. He joined a debating society, for which his grandfather paid the initiation fee, and won a gold medal, learning a "readiness in composition and facility in expressing his thoughts," two valuable assets for any young man.

In the early winter of 1845, James was back under Mr. Bartlett's tutelage at the Collegiate School, presumably only for special tutoring, as by the fall of 1846 the records of Union College in Schenectady show that he was a student in advanced standing. The Reverend Mr. Cuyler of the Dutch Reformed Church may have turned his parents' thoughts to Union, or James may have enrolled there simply because it had a reputation as the best senior college in America. In those days students could enroll at college for one or two terms only, and could transfer from one institution to another without much difficulty over grades or credits.

Union College was then over sixty years old, and flourishing mightily under the presidency of that extraordinary man of God, of learning and practical science, the great Eliphalet Nott. Dr. Nott was credited with patents on thirty different kinds of stoves; he invented an anthracite-burning boiler for steamboats which virtually did away with boiler explosions; and he introduced the first engineering course connected with a general college.

At the same time, he held the chair of Moral Philosophy and taught the most popular course on the college campus in that subject. In some way, this course appeared to contain the formula for success in practical leadership, and students thronged to hear him. He must have had a tremendous and decisive influence on most of the young men who attended his lectures, and James Roosevelt could have been no exception.

What, precisely, were the precepts which Dr. Nott handed down to his audiences for more than half a century?

He himself said that his own avowed purpose was to give the mind, the spirit, and the moral nature of a student that inspiration which should enable him when he came into the stress of life to show that he was competent to do the work that he was sent to do. He told his students that every man can be really great if he will trust his own high instinct, think his own thought, and say his own word. He endeavored, he said, to make men rather than scholars; he urged his students to form a plan or purpose in life. "Search your own minds," he told them, "turn your thoughts upon some design or course of life that will entertain you with hopes. Mark out a laudable course of conduct, so will you go through life acquiring power and influence over men."

This giant among inspirational speakers was already seventy-three years of age when James Roosevelt entered Union. But the flash of his personality and the cadences in his trained orator's voice were as powerful as ever. His listeners heard him roll out his sentences, and a great deal of his thinking, his counsel and admonitions must have taken root in their hearts and minds.

"You are approaching," he told the senior class, "that period when you must enter upon the great world. If ever you would be men, you must learn to be so now. The best instruction is gained from our own thoughts as well as from experience; for though a man may grow learned by another man's thoughts, yet he will grow wise and happy only by his own."

This was the fare spread before James, and he received inestimable nourishment from it. For he was the kind of young man whose character Dr. Nott delighted in forming and upon whom he lavished his most sympathetic efforts.

It must have been all the more painful for the educator, therefore, to have to write to Dr. Isaac Roosevelt that his son had entered into a secret society, contrary to the laws of the college, and, what was worse, a society which held its meetings at a tavern. This may have been the Greek-letter fraternity Delta Phi, which had already been in existence at Union for twenty years, and which had Dr. Nott's blessing as a social organization. It must have been the tavern which set off such sparks of educational and parental indignation.

Without further upset, James finished his studies in the spring term of 1847, although the college records show that he did not receive his degree until 1848. However, he did not return to Union in the fall of 1847, for by that time his family was once again in an upheaval, trying to make up Dr. Isaac's mind to send his son on the Grand Tour (of Europe), fashionably undertaken at that time by the offspring of wealthy families in the United States.

Grandfather James had died in February, at a hale eighty-eight, after suffering a stroke. New York, declared the press, had lost a gentleman of the old school. His home, Mount Hope, was left to James, although the grandson did not occupy it until some years later. It seems not to have been a lack of funds, or any question of the suitability of a European tour as a means of completing an education, which deterred Dr. Isaac from making up his mind about his boy's immediate future; but rather the fear of his becoming ill on

the voyage, or even of his dying. For Dr. Isaac believed that
it was the great business of this life to be prepared for another and better world, into which one might be thrust
without an instant's warning, and frequently reminded his
son that "we know not what a day may bring forth. 'Be ye
also ready' is the warning voice."

Morbidly preoccupied with this true but uncomforting
philosophy, Dr. Isaac found it almost impossible to part with
his first-born for a great length of time and to send him a
vast distance, perhaps never to see him again. An autograph
letter from Mrs. Dr. Isaac to her husband, undated, but
written while this struggle over James' immediate future
was tormenting them all, sheds light on what the poor
woman must have had to endure from her husband's vacil-
lation and indecisiveness. She was in New York, at the bedside of her father, who was seriously ill, and who died in the
first week of October 1847.

To Dr. Isaac she wrote: ". . . I think so much of my dear
James, and last night while sitting by my Father's bedside,
my thoughts were with him. I do hope *sincerely* you will
allow him to go, and it is my opinion if there is no other way
opened, it is best for him to go to Mr. Sergeants and leave
him in the hands of our Heavenly Father and if our lives
are spared we will join him in the Spring. But my dear husband, I am still willing to abide by your decision for then I
shall be perfectly satisfied for *you* will then be happy but let
us lay aside our own selfish feelings for the good of our dear
child.

"Love to dear James and Johnny, I know James will be a
comfort to you. John [her brother] says he had a very satisfactory and pleasant talk with him night before last."

It is of record that a passport, signed by James Buchanan,
then Secretary of State, was issued to Mr. James Roosevelt

on September 29, 1847. The bearer is described as five feet eight inches tall, with a round forehead, rather thin face, hazel eyes, dark hair, a straight nose, and a round chin. His age is given as twenty-one, which was a slight liberty with the truth, for at that date Mr. James Roosevelt was barely turned nineteen. Passports were not issued to minors.

It was now too late to put off a decision. Mrs. Roosevelt's suggestion was followed, and the harassed Dr. Isaac finally consented to let his son leave his native shores in company with the Mr. Sergeant mentioned in the letter.

The probability is that this gentleman, whose name is spelled variously Sergeant, Sargent, and Sargeant, was the friend and neighbor of Mr. Andrew Jackson Downing, of whose estate, Wodenethe, near Fishkill Landing, Mr. Downing wrote with enthusiasm. Mr. Downing referred in 1850 to the fact that Mr. H. W. Sargent had just passed a couple of years abroad, "curiously gleaning all clever foreign notions that were really worth naturalizing at home. . . . Wodenethe," further continued Mr. Downing, "is a *bijou* full of interest for the lover of rural beauty, abounding in rare trees, shrubs and plants, as well as vases, and objects of rural embellishment of all kinds."

Presumably in company with this studious and cultured gentleman of Fishkill Landing, James Roosevelt set forth to see the world at nineteen—a college career behind him, his purse cautiously filled by his father, a firm heredity of good sense tempering the natural curiosity and adventurous spirit of youth and youthful virility.

He traveled through Europe from November 1847 until May 1849, enjoying the sights of London and Paris, laying the foundation for future friendships with young gentlemen of his own age and class, particularly in England. An excursion into Italy was a "must" on the Grand Tour. No American visiting Europe in the eighteen-forties would have thought of omitting the classical scenes of Rome, the damp mustiness of Venice, and the blue of the Bay of Naples.

Dr. Isaac was, of course, overjoyed that his son was absorbing such cultural advantages, but the danger of thieves and brigands in out-of-the-way Italian villages, the likelihood of James' suffering undue fatigue as the result of his long journeys by stage and chaise, worried his father dreadfully. When James decided, early in 1848, to include the Holy Land in his itinerary, poor Dr. Isaac was really distraught. He delighted in the thought of his son's visiting the geographical location of Christianity's birth, but he dreaded the prospect of James exposed to malaria on the coast of Syria and wandering with fevered brow among the ruins of dilapidated cities.

If the story told in the Roosevelt family is true, it was in Italy that James allowed himself the one great fling of his career. His son Franklin used to relate that his father and a companion (Mr. Sargent?) decided that it would be an adventure to join with Garibaldi, at that time the bold fighter for Italy's unification and freedom against the Papal States. The years 1848 and 1849 were a period, it must be remembered, when the burning topic of freedom was everywhere in the European atmosphere. For a month, according to the tale, James and his liberty-loving American friend trained in a soldiers' camp, as members of Garibaldi's Legion. It turned out to be a month of stalemate for freedom's forces, however, and after thirty days of boredom both young men decided that they had had enough of heroism and inaction, and gave up soldiering.

Dr. Isaac expressed great relief when his son left Italy for Munich, and pointed out that liberty in Europe was far different from the liberty enjoyed in the United States. Furthermore, he hoped that James would take no active part in the revolutions which were agitating the Old World.

However, James was in Naples in March 1849, at a time when Garibaldi the Liberator was encamped in the border town of Rieti, in the face of his enemy, King Ferdinand of Naples. It makes a provocative picture—the quiet, conservative young scion of Hudson River aristocracy, garbed in a red blouse, wearing a high-crowned Calabrian hat with an ostrich feather floating from it, spurring his horse on the Liberator's errands.

Against this romantic possibility must be set the fact that Dr. Isaac had finally screwed his courage to the sticking point, and after several false starts had reserved passage for himself and his wife on a steamer leaving New York for England on October 11, 1848. The plan was to unite the family in Paris, and then proceed to the south of Europe, as the Doctor always found cold dampness injurious to his health. Would James have joined Garibaldi if his father were in Europe? The evidence that the Isaac Roosevelts actually crossed the ocean is all too scanty.

Reading between the lines, it is possible to assume that James may have been with his parents during the winter, if they did arrive, and upon their departure may have returned to make his gallant gesture for freedom. One can only speculate—but what must Dr. Isaac have suffered, if the story is actually authentic!

As a matter of cold truth, the most positively identified mementos of James' Italian trip are three "little spindly chairs," now placed in the living room of the Hyde Park home. Mrs. James Roosevelt mentioned these in 1931, and added that there were three others either in the old Sargent place or at the Howland place in New Hamburg.

By spring of 1849, James Roosevelt had been in Europe

some eighteen months. He had visited France, England, Spain, Italy, Germany, Greece, and the Holy Land, traveling, in compliance with his father's wishes, as a gentleman should. He had gazed upon the masterpieces of classical art in all the great galleries in the capitals of Europe, and had considered purchasing paintings to bring home with him. He was presumably "finished" and his academic education completed in most suitable style. With his family connections, there were innumerable opportunities open to him in the business world. But apparently he felt that he had not yet found the design or course of life that Dr. Nott had said would entertain him with hope.

A possible reason for this attitude may lie in the fact that Mr. Benjamin Douglas Silliman, one of the most prominent members of the bar in New York City, made a trip to Europe in 1848. No documentary evidence has as yet come to light to indicate that he met and talked with twenty-year-old James Roosevelt during his travels. The fact that James later became a law clerk in Mr. Silliman's office may be purely coincidental.

The Roosevelt name was entered upon the books of the Harvard Law School as of November 15, 1849. The young gentleman who had lately traversed the dangerous Italian roads with a courier, now settled down at Mr. Daily's in Cambridge. Here he applied himself to the pursuit of Blackstone and Kent, and all that formidable array of English common law from which American jurisprudence is so largely descended.

In those days the rigors of a winter at Mr. Daily's must have been formidable. Room rent for students (from twenty-six to fifty-two dollars for a term of twenty weeks) did not include fuel, and the college announced that fuel prepared for use would be furnished by the lessee of the college wharf at market price. A servant to "make fires, etc." cost from five to ten dollars a term. Board for the twenty weeks ran from two dollars to two-fifty a week, and washing from seven dollars to fifteen dollars for the same period.

The roster of one hundred students was instructed by three professors. One may safely assume that these gentlemen had none of them the ringing eloquence of Dr. Eliphalet Nott; but they taught their students amply in the law. James Roosevelt received his LL.B. from Harvard on his twenty-third birthday. The banks of Boston closed for Harvard Commencement, and there was a Commencement dinner served in Harvard Hall, but, alcoholic beverages having been prohibited on this occasion some five years before, only water and lemonade were consumed. The Boston *Courier* complained that Commencement, which used to be such a "great time," had diminished in importance as a popular festival, and that few people came to stare their eyes out on Cambridge Common, where there was no more sucking of egg-nog.

One last touch of ritual and color was left. The Sheriff of Middlesex County opened Commencement by advancing to the front of the platform and, striking the floor three times with his sword in its scabbard, uttered the command, "The meeting will be in order."

Immediately upon graduation James was admitted to the bar. He entered Mr. Silliman's office, and at once found himself in a position to obtain the widest variety of legal experience. Mr. Silliman pleaded in the state courts, the federal courts, and the Supreme Court of the United States. His practice embraced common, equity, and admiralty law; and his clients included many large and important corporations.

The swiftness with which the young man advanced in his career more than vindicated his youthful reputation for steadiness and reliability. One year out of Law School, he was elected a director of the Consolidated Coal Company of

Maryland. This was the company, it should be borne in mind, in which Mr. Warren Delano of Newburgh also held important interests. It appears to have been James' first taste of business and finance, and he found it to his liking. Within a short time he withdrew from the practice of law and occupied all his energies with the management of banks and transportation companies.

The Roosevelts had been among the first to invest in railroad stocks. Grandfather James, shortly before his death in 1847, attended a "large and respectable meeting of the citizens of Poughkeepsie in favor of the speedy construction of the Hudson River Railroad" and subscribed five thousand dollars. Matthew Vassar, Esq., founder of Vassar College, was chairman of this meeting. By 1848 Dr. Isaac also had "full stock" in the Railroad Company, having paid five thousand dollars in full. He held Delaware and Hudson stock as well, and although he permitted himself mild jokes about the railroad not being able to run uphill as well as down, he thought sufficiently well of the new venture to override his native caution and become a substantial stockholder.

It was natural, therefore, for James to invest in and work with the railroad companies, which were, in the middle of the nineteenth century, spreading the iron web of their tracks all up and down and across the eastern seaboard. Following his affiliation with the Consolidated Coal Company, he became general manager of the Cumberland and Pennsylvania Railroad, and was thus fully established as a railroad and financial entrepreneur.

At twenty-five, already financially independent and the owner of Mount Hope and its many fruitful acres, James Roosevelt was ready to consider matrimony. Aside from a little gentle teasing from his Grandmother Roosevelt about playing gallant to the young ladies, and a fleeting reference to a Miss Hamilton in England, James seems not to have become seriously embroiled with romance until he fell in love with Miss Rebecca Howland. Miss Howland was of that family which had already furnished two Roosevelt brides—his Grandfather James' last wife, and his Grandfather Aspinwall's spouse. She was the daughter of Mr. Gardiner Greene Howland, the same who had feared lest the University of New York make a dandy of James. That made her his mother's first cousin, although there was a difference of twenty-two years between the two.

According to all reports, she was plump and pretty and possessed of such vivacious humor and bounce as to make her both popular and attractive. They were married in 1853, and in 1855 she bore James Roosevelt a son, christened James Roosevelt Roosevelt but called from his earliest years by the euphonious nickname of "Rosy."

There was a delightful continuity about the life of the Roosevelt family on the Hudson. Each oldest son of his generation married and begot a son, so that the years flowed on with few sudden and startling changes. There were summer days spent boating on the river, or driving out to friends. There were winter days on the ice, with iceboating and sleighing, and usually a month or two in New York City during the bitterest weather. The crops were bountiful; there were always good horses in the stables, and carriages for the ladies. The Roosevelts belonged to that society of New York families which had position and prestige because they were old and well established. They were not "fashionable" in Mrs. William Astor's sense of the word, for they had no need to be. They did not buy two-hundred-thousand-dollar houses at Newport, as she did, or wear eight hundred thousand dollars' worth of diamonds out to afternoon tea parties, as the newspapers accused her mother-in-law of doing.

They were ladies and gentlemen with sufficient means to

live comfortable and pleasant lives; their investments were conservative, and they lived complacently within their ample incomes. A home in New York and a home on the Hudson (preferably the east bank), a trip abroad every now and then—if these demands were satisfied they asked no more. There was no political discontent or ferment, no striving after office, no loud publicity about their comings and goings. Quietly and competently they managed their charities, their business affairs, and their pleasures.

James Roosevelt was cut precisely to this pattern. The most even-tempered and courteous of men, he won the regard of his business associates with his scrupulously honest dealings and fairness, and in his thirties already began to be thought of around Hyde Park and Poughkeepsie as young Squire Roosevelt.

As for travel, remembering the congenial society in England, Mr. Roosevelt frequently visited his friends in that country with Mrs. Roosevelt and their boy. They were there in 1861, and in 1865, a few weeks after Lee's surrender, they sailed again.

Although he was of an age to do so, James Roosevelt did not join the Union Army, but it is said that he worked for the Northern cause through that incredible and valiant movement, the Sanitary Commission. A search of the roster of commissioners and agents has failed to reveal his name; but the activities of this agency were so complicated and varied that it is entirely possible he may have rendered yeoman service and yet his deeds remained unsung.

The Sanitary Commission, a precursor of the Red Cross, had originally been formed to assist the Medical Bureau of the War Department in improving the condition of Army camps and to make suggestions which would better the lot of the sick and wounded soldier. Before the war ended, the Sanitary Commission, under the chairmanship of Dr. Henry

Bellows, the Unitarian clergyman of New York and friend of the Warren Delanos, had taken charge of the instruction of Army surgeons and physicians, of transfer of prisoners, of messages to and about men serving in the Army; of leaves granted to soldiers, and of all contributions to soldiers in the way of food, clothing, luxuries, and so on, to mention only a few of its functions.

There were five or six great Sanitary fairs held in cities throughout the country for the purpose of raising money for this commission, which was entirely financed by voluntary contributions; and even small Poughkeepsie, a town of less than twenty thousand inhabitants, made over sixteen thousand dollars at a fair which was the talk of Dutchess County for many a long day. Mrs. Dr. Roosevelt gave six dollars toward the fair, but appears not to have visited in person.

It would have been more likely that James Roosevelt, with his ever surer finger on the pulse of the nation's railroads, made his contribution to the cause in which he believed by assisting the government with its transportation problems. In view of the energy with which he later attacked the tangled question of restoring the railroads of the South to something like their prewar efficiency, this would appear to be a reasonable surmise.

The reconstruction of the railroads below the Mason-Dixon line was not undertaken until 1871; and in the years between the end of the war and that date Mr. James Roosevelt found himself very fully occupied in Dutchess County.

During the summer of 1866, when he and his wife and young son were traveling in England and France, Mount Hope was rented to a family from New York City. In some inexplicable manner the house caught fire, and despite every effort made to save it, the old homestead was almost entirely destroyed by fire.

Franklin Roosevelt told the story of the fire, prefixing it

with his significant "as rumor has it," to the effect that the
butler in the tenants' establishment became thoroughly bored
with country life and, wishing to return to the city, thought
he could solve his problem by setting fire to the house.

Whatever the origin, the results were certainly disastrous.
Family papers were burned, among them many of James'
personal letters; many family records were also destroyed;
and a large part of the fine furniture and furnishings which
had been willed to James Roosevelt by his grandfather James
was irreparably lost. Some few items were rescued, among
them the dining-room chairs with the family arms carved on
the back, two small Duncan Phyfe chairs, a large silver tea
service, period of George II, which had belonged to Isaac
the Patriot, and the rosewood bed and bureau now in the
Pink Room of the Franklin D. Roosevelt Home at Hyde
Park.

Some other items were salvaged from the ruins of Mount
Hope's cellar, and the story about them again has a "rumor
has it" prefix. As Franklin Roosevelt told it, there had been a
ghost at Mount Hope for a long, long time, a ghost which
delighted in waking visitors with great crashing noises,
rather as if stone cannon balls were being rolled down the
marble stairs. Many people claimed to have heard this
racket, including Mr. James Roosevelt, and they all said that
it sounded as if the ball were started from the top step,
gathered momentum, and landed with a crash in the main
hall. After the fire, three stone cannon balls were found in
the cellar. Franklin Roosevelt would end the story with,
"That's all there is to it."

Ghost or no ghost, it now became imperative for Mr. and
Mrs. James Roosevelt to find another home. Meeting, at last,
that Maker before whom he had trembled for so many years,
Dr. Isaac died in 1863. Obituaries again referred to a Roosevelt as "a gentleman of the old school." His son John had

been married in June to Miss Ellen Murray Crosby of Pough-keepsie, so Rosedale could not be a permanent refuge. James naturally wished to have a home of his own, particularly since he had become deeply interested in breeding good horses—as his grandfather had been before him—and felt that he must have proper stables.

Then as now, the problem of buying a house bristled with difficulties. The Roosevelts were determined to remain near the Hudson, and estates of appropriate size and elegance were, even for that day, very expensive. It was said that Mr. Roosevelt approached John Jacob Astor to see whether he could not buy his estate, Ferncliff, at Rhinebeck, but that he thought the price, fifty thousand dollars, was too steep. Eventually, after a great deal of driving out and looking and walking over grounds and inspecting houses, the Roosevelts decided upon the Josiah Wheeler place in Hyde Park. It was about two miles north of Rosedale, on the same side of the Post Road, with lands running steeply through a wooded bank to the river, and an old house, built some forty years before, standing well back from the highway. The dwelling was clapboarded, with the familiar Hudson River brackets under the eaves, an open porch running along the south-east side, and a tower on the southeast corner. It did not qualify for the title of mansion in any degree, but the Roose-velts thought they could make it comfortable, and there was ample space for Mr. Roosevelt's trotting horses.

There was also a charming old garden, laid out about 1830, enclosed by a tall hemlock hedge, in which roses and perennials and fruit trees flourished.

Springwood, as they decided to call their home, has al-ways had wonderful roses, and the very first summer the Roosevelts were there, it was said that they picked "thou-sands of roses before breakfast."

The deed was signed and "everything paid for" by early

June 1867, although the moving had been accomplished and workmen put to renovating all during the month of May. New bedroom furniture was bought, new carpet was sewed, new oilcloth was laid down, and new plumbing was installed; and by the end of July the Roosevelts were comfortably settled at Springwood.

At that time there was on the first floor of the house an entrance hall, a dining room on the west, looking toward the Hudson, a southwest drawing room or music room, with gray silk draperies and valances, a library, and the South Parlor, the east end of which is now the small room known as the Snuggery. The South Parlor, then as now, was darkly furnished and darkly lighted, for vines grew thickly on the pillars of the wide veranda outside. The pantries, kitchen, and laundry were at the north end of the house.

Upstairs there was a large master bedroom on the southeast, from which an upstairs sitting room opened; a bathroom; and four other bedrooms. The tower on the southeast afforded a schoolroom and playroom on the third floor.

In the style of the day, the furnishings were dark walnut and rosewood, with "Turkey carpets" and Brussels carpet on the floors.

Mr. Roosevelt superintended all the work himself. When he had got matters going well at the house, he had his Alderney cows to see to, and the stables for the driving horses, as well as the barn directly below the hill, which was to be used for the brood mares.

But he would not have been a Roosevelt if he had been content merely to lead the life of a country gentleman on the forty-odd acres of Springwood, with nothing growing about him but flowers and a few vegetables for his own table. He wished to carry on farming actively, as his father and grandfather had done before him, and in 1868 he bought from Robert Boreel another 234 acres, adjoining Springwood on the south.

In the years after the settling in, Mr. Roosevelt led a full and active life. Having moved into the township of Hyde Park from the township of Poughkeepsie, he began to take an active part in community activities.

He was elected Supervisor of the town of Hyde Park for two years (1871–1873) on the Democratic ticket. In that capacity he administered town affairs and by virtue of this office also sat on the Dutchess County Board of Supervisors. A perusal of the minutes of this board discloses that Supervisor Roosevelt was ever watchful of the taxpayers' money. As a member of the committee to authorize repairs and alterations on public buildings, he succeeded in holding the total cost for such repairs and improvements down to $74.84. He reduced the payment of supervisors for "footing the tax rolls" from $6 to $4. He further moved that no supervisor of the board should be allowed his per diem of $3 for any day that the board was not actually in session. He served on a committee for the improvement of conditions at the county jail, when aroused citizens complained by petition that criminals under sentence, innocent witnesses, and persons charged with crime were confined together, and that the contiguity between the male and female apartments was productive of injurious results. The petitioners, prominent members of the community, protested that such conditions were calculated to degrade the innocent in their own esteem, to demoralize them and make them vicious by compulsory association with condemned criminals. The Supervisors' Committee investigated, and some improvements were made.

Mr. Roosevelt interested himself in the public schools of Hyde Park, and was chiefly instrumental in having a new red brick schoolhouse erected on the main street of the

village (part of the Albany Post Road), at the corner of
Harvey Street, on a spot now occupied by a gasoline station.
This was a model building for its day, two-storied, with
high-ceilinged classrooms on each floor and tall, narrow
windows. Kerosene lamps and iron coal stoves furnished
light and heat. There were eight grades, and two years of
high school.

Some of Hyde Park's oldest citizens can recall that Mr.
Roosevelt was the only taxpayer in the village who was concerned enough to visit the school month after month, and
that he always sat beside the teacher's desk on the raised
platform and listened to a recitation or two. "Medium tall,
he was, with a good-size calf. He wore mutton chops and he
was a gen-u-wine farmer." An accurate description, for it
is a matter of record in the family that James took to wearing side-whiskers in the eighteen-fifties, and he continued
that hirsute adornment until his death.

It was not until the eighties that he found the time to sit
regularly on the school board and attend the monthly meetings. His duties as one of the members of the Board of Man-
agers of the Hudson River State Hospital, which he faithfully carried out, beginning in 1873 and for more than
twenty years thereafter, also took his time and attention
when he was able to be in Hyde Park. The institution,
known colloquially in that day as the State Lunatic Asylum,
had been built immediately south of the site of old Mount
Hope. When the latter burned, the Roosevelts decided to
sell the land to the state for forty-five thousand dollars,
although it did cost them a wrench "to sell their loved
home to the State." Not only because of his kindly interest
in the unfortunate, but perhaps for old association's sake as
well, Mr. Roosevelt made frequent visits to the "Asylum."
The inspection entries of the board indicate that he would
visit all the wards as well as the utility rooms. For instance,

on June 18, 1873, he noted: "Ward 8 over-crowded, twenty-eight in this ward intended for fifteen. . . . The Hospital in excellent condition and patients well cared for. Number in the house, women 87, men 85. James Roosevelt, Manager."

It was at this time, too, that the reorganization of the Southern railroads was occupying him most fully. He was serving as president of the Southern Railway Security Company, the purpose of which was to secure control of such Southern railroads as were essential to the formation of through lines between New York, Philadelphia, Baltimore, Washington, and the principal cities of the South. He felt it was essential to bring new economic life to the stricken Confederate States and to establish their numerous and disorganized railroads upon a sound, working, business basis. These affairs naturally took him away from Hyde Park frequently and occupied his energies almost exclusively.

In 1875 he was elected to the board of the Delaware and Hudson Railroad, a post he continued to hold throughout his life and an association of increasing importance.

This company was originally known as the Delaware and Hudson Canal Company's Railroad. The canal itself had been built in 1828 to carry coal from the mines of Pennsylvania to the Hudson River at Rondout. James Roosevelt had been vice-president and general manager of the water-borne transportation system, and when, with the development of rail transportation, the company added various small railroad lines to its holdings, it was only natural that he should sit on the board and continue to assist on the management level. With what success he did so can be observed by the following brief extract from the minutes of a meeting of the Board of Directors immediately after his death.

"Mr. Roosevelt's varied practical experience fitted him to be most useful and effective in the affairs of the Company and during his connection therewith he gave continuous and careful attention to its interests. As questions arose with reference thereto, he familiarized himself thoroughly with their merits, and although he did not shun responsibility when necessary, his inclination was always toward a wise conservatism such as he deemed would aid the permanent prosperity of the Company. His services to it were, therefore, most valuable in their character. In addition to this, Mr. Roosevelt was always most urbane and considerate in his personal relations. While he had no hesitation in expressing his view as to matters of sound policy, no element of personal feeling ever resulted from any difference of opinion. To each member of the Board he was a most agreeable and esteemed personal friend."

By 1875 Rebecca Roosevelt's health began to give cause for concern. Signs of a heart ailment appeared, which did not yield to treatment, but on the contrary showed signs of becoming more and more serious. In the summer of 1876 she was in very poor health. A yachting excursion up Long Island Sound was planned for her, in order that she might take what benefit she could from the sea air; but before the voyage was fairly under way she became so ill that her husband was obliged to put back and take her to 15 Washington Square.

Here she died on August 31. The obituary account in the Poughkeepsie *Daily Eagle,* which said her death would "cast a gloom among many who loved her for her kind heart and other endearing qualities," could only hint at the grief of her family and friends, of her son and her husband. She was buried in the churchyard of St. James Church in Hyde Park—the merry wife of James Roosevelt's youth, who had brimmed with vivacity and humor and who had been overjoyed at picking "thousands of roses before breakfast."

Two years after her death, Rosy, her twenty-one-year-old son, made what Europeans refer to as a good *parti.* He married Helen Schermerhorn Astor, granddaughter of John Jacob Astor, and niece of Laura Astor Delano, who with her husband, the Delanos' dear "Uncle Frank," entertained the Delano girls so frequently.

Mr. James Roosevelt, at fifty years of age, was left to live alone in Springwood, the house which he and Rebecca Roosevelt had had such difficulty deciding upon, and which, after they moved in, had given them both so much pleasure. It was not that his was a lonely widowerhood; his extensive acquaintance in New York City, and his many interests there and on the banks of the Hudson, obviated any danger of a flat, empty, or insipid life. But a roomy old clapboard house for one lone gentleman seemed very big. Business trips around the country could be tedious, always undertaken alone; and any European visits embarked upon singly only emphasized the loss of Rebecca Howland's warm humor and lovable companionship. He was a practical and sensible man, but also gentle, kind, and sensitive. This tragedy of his middle age must have struck hard and deep.

His friends sensed his loneliness, for they received him in their homes even more cordially than in the past. He was a popular guest and no doubt was paired off with an eligible lady by more than one hostess.

Even so, it must have come as a surprise to many when the poised and cultured Miss Sara Delano moved with easy grace into the vacuum of his personal life.

Within a few weeks of that fragrant week in May 1880 (up to that date the hottest May on record in the Hudson Valley), Mr. James Roosevelt arrived at Algonac from Hyde Park at eleven in the morning and stayed until the following noon. Almost immediately thereafter Sister Dora and her husband, Will Forbes, went to visit at Hyde Park and stayed five days. Two weeks later, on a very warm day, Mr. Roosevelt stopped off at Algonac on his way up from New York.

Mr. Delano had known James Roosevelt for many years. He had sat with him on boards of various enterprises, and planned policies and management with him. They belonged to the same clubs and shared the same views—except in politics. Mr. Roosevelt, although he had temporarily left the fold of the Democratic party during the Civil War, had swung back again; and Warren Delano, whose remarks about Democrats were superlatively uncomplimentary. admitted grudgingly that Mr. Roosevelt was a living proof that a man could be a Democrat *and* a gentleman. But when this exceptional Democrat asked for Sallie's hand in marriage, her Papa, so it is said, made strong demurrals. What father would not have done so? Sallie was not quite twenty-six; her suitor was fifty-two, with a son just six months younger than she. Yet who could resist a man of such quiet charm, such obvious breeding and refinement, such courtesy, such warmth, such business and financial standing?

By early summer it was tacitly understood that "Sallie and Mr. R.," as they were familiarly referred to at Algonac, would be married in the fall. Plans for a large wedding were already afoot; but by the first of August, poor Auntie's invalid condition had become so much worse that she wrung her brother's heart as she lay in her bed, a picture of utter weakness and exhaustion. Eleven days later she slipped into unconsciousness and then into death.

There could now be no thought of a large and elaborate wedding. Aside from any feeling of punctiliousness about mourning (and the Delanos and Roosevelts were very punctilious about it), Sallie could not have endured the thought of disrespect to the memory of the beloved aunt whose name she bore. So a date was set in October, and only the immediate families and closest friends were invited to attend. Mr. Roosevelt was now, of course, accepted as a member of the Algonac family and made many trips back and forth between Newburgh and Hyde Park. Sallie went with him to New York to call upon Mr. Gardiner Howland, the father of Rebecca; and various Delanos, including Uncle Ned, went to stay at Hyde Park.

That was the year when roses bloomed early and profusely because of the heat; when the horse-chestnut blossoms, with their beautiful pink tints, made the roads between Hyde Park and Algonac a bower of rosy foam. Strawberries were early, plentiful, and cheap—twenty cents a quart. A local fisherman from Hyde Park caught a black bass in the Hudson weighing over a hundred pounds. The ax factory in that village burned, at a loss of five thousand dollars.

Because of the continued heat and drought, the water in the Hudson grew so brackish toward the end of the summer that the locomotive engineers complained about it. The timothy crop was feared for, and cattle began to suffer. A disease among the horses of the region, called the "epizootic," broke out and made the animals snuffle and cough, causing much concern. And in the early fall people's minds turned toward the coming presidential election.

The Republicans came to Warren Delano for aid, and the Democrats on the other side of the river, in Poughkeepsie, offered the Democratic nomination for Congress to James Roosevelt. He refused it, of course. In the same newspaper column in which a note of this fact appeared was the comment, " 'Lemme see,' say the Democratic leaders here, 'who shall we run for Congress?' Then someone mentions a name and immediately there is a chorus of voices, 'How's he fixed?' "

The supporters of Garfield and Arthur put on a crashing torchlight parade in Newburgh, with bands and rockets and Roman candles and huge banners, which the Democrats pelted with rotten eggs.

A band of gypsies, with sixty wagons and teams, camped

near Newburgh, and James Gordon Bennett's yacht, the *Polynia,* steamed up the river. The Delanos went aboard her before she was put into the docks for overhauling.

A week before Sara Delano's wedding the girls in the cotton factory at Newburgh went on strike. They earned $4.50 a week and demanded $5.00.

By the fifth of October wedding presents were beginning to pour in—lovely mustard pots, and cut-glass candlesticks, table services, silver, articles of virtu, heirlooms, and art treasures. Nelly Blodgett came from New York and helped Kassie and Warren III's wife, Jennie, to gather wild flowers for decorations. The gardeners were hard at work, filling the house with plants and flowers, raking leaves outdoors, and cleaning up about the grounds.

Harriet Wood had already gone to Springwood with the bride's trousseau, and had laid out her clothes in the bureau drawers and black walnut wardrobe of the southeast bedroom.

Papa, anxious to have everything just so for the wedding, on the very morning of October 7, the wedding day, put a carpenter and a painter to work on last-minute touches.

The New York *World* carried a fairly accurate description of the festivities. "The relatives and friends from New York," it announced, "were met with carriages at the ferry landing. The drive to Algonac lies through some of the most picturesque woodland scenery on the Hudson and many of the villagers and residents in the pretty country cottages on the roadside turned out to do honor to the wedding guests.

"The interior of the house was handsomely decorated in every style of horticultural art by Mr. Delano's gardener. At the right of the entrance are two library rooms in which Mr. and Mrs. Delano with their two unmarried daughters Kassie and Laura received the wedding guests and relatives.

Across the vestibule is the drawing room in which the marriage ceremony took place, and which for this special occasion was made into a conservatory filled with the choicest plants and flowers. The rear wall of an alcove on the west side of the room was metamorphosed into a floral chancel whose foundation was composed of ferns and tropical palms, the walls having been carefully marked by garlands of trailing ivy. At precisely 2:30 P.M. [actually 3 o'clock, as trains were late] Dr. Bellows of New York appeared under this floral canopy and began reading the marriage service. There were no bridesmaids, but the sisters and female relatives of the bridegroom stood with the bridal party."

The New York *Times* mentioned the bride's costume, which was of pure white brocade, worn with a tulle veil, unbroken by any trace of color except that of the bridal bouquet. The neck was high in back with a rolling collar which displayed to advantage the five-strand pearl necklace—gift of the bridegroom.

It was a beautiful October day, bright and cheerful, and the ripening foliage was brilliant in the autumn sunlight —a real wedding day, it seemed to those who watched Dr. Bellows unite Sara Delano and James Roosevelt in holy matrimony. Mrs. Dr. Isaac Roosevelt was there, in black silk, to see her son married to this tall, dark bride; Mr. John Aspinwall Roosevelt and his wife were there. Their young daughters, Grace and Ellen, were also present (the latter remembers that Aunt Sallie made a lovely bride, and her sister Kassie was lovely, too), Rosy Roosevelt and Helen Astor Roosevelt, Bammie Roosevelt, and the Joseph Howlands (James' cousins). Mrs. Howland remembered many years afterward how proud and happy dear James looked, and "what a beautiful wedding it was!"

The A. A. Lows, the Hitches, Uncle Frank and Aunt

Laura Delano, and others, made up the one hundred and twenty-five relatives and friends who stood in the drawing room and heard the marriage service read.

Afterward the guests repaired to the dining room, where a "collation had been laid" by the renowned caterer Pinard. And at twenty minutes past four, Papa noted, the married pair left the house in the Delano victoria, drawn by Mag and Pet and driven by French, the coachman.

Mrs. James Roosevelt's going-away costume was of gray, trimmed with black, with a small round black hat, half-mourning in deference to the memory of Nannie and Aunt Sarah. But there could have been no mourning in her heart, for she was the newly married bride of the man who would always be her "dear James."

Halfway to Hyde Park, on the west bank of the Hudson, James Roosevelt's coachman, Hutchins, met the bridal pair with a T-cart. Mr. Roosevelt himself took the reins, and in the flashing October sunlight, with the Hudson shining below them and such a tang in the air as comes only in the Hudson Valley, James and Sara Roosevelt drove to Poughkeepsie by way of the Highland ferry, up the Albany Post Road, past the hill on which Mount Hope had stood, past the gates of Rosedale, and down the wonderful lane of trees leading to Springwood, their home.

IV

James and Sara Roosevelt

OCTOBER is the most beautiful month of all the year throughout the Hudson Valley. It is not alone the bright sunlight or the flamboyance of the hillsides as the leaves begin to color. It is not even the brilliance of the blue sky, or the faint smell of burning wood and leaves which always hangs in the atmosphere. It is a combination of all these, to which is added a special feeling in the air, not sharp, not soft, not hot, not cold, but a wonderful blending of all the pleasant things that air can be. There is a radiant serenity about October in Dutchess County which charms the summer residents into lingering and makes it difficult for the year-round inhabitants to go away from home. Dutchess County in October is the perfect honeymoon spot.

Mr. James Roosevelt felt it to be so. And his bride, whose earliest memories were of the Hudson too, was more than content to spend a month in her new home in Hyde Park before they left on a second Grand Tour, which should include that part of Europe which they both knew, and other scenes which should be pleasantly strange to both of them.

Curiously enough, on the night of October 7, 1880, there was in Hyde Park a skimelton, the good old country greeting to newlyweds. According to ancient custom, the friends of the bride and groom, arming themselves with tin pans, pot lids, kettles, and other makeshift noise-makers, surround the home of the happy pair, crashing and banging, making the night hideous with the noise of metal. Custom decrees that the rude serenaders be invited in to partake of cake and cider (in the fall) and that the wedded couple join in the fun.

This skimelton, however, did not intrude upon the privacy of Mr. and Mrs. James Roosevelt. It was held to honor a Mr. and Mrs. James Devine.

For the first week after their wedding the Roosevelts roamed quietly over their own grounds, going to the stables to see to the horses, looking in at the greenhouses and the grapery, inspecting the farm. There was a daily ride on horseback, and then a row upon the river in the wherry, usually down to Rosedale, where they called upon Mrs. Dr. Isaac, or to see Brother John and his family. Mrs. Roosevelt has been described on these short nautical outings as wearing a *trotteur,* or walking costume, of black or gray serge, dabbling her fingers in the water as her husband took the oars and pulled the boat quietly along beside the bank.

There would hardly have been time or inclination, during this splendid outdoor month, for Mrs. Roosevelt to have made many changes in the house at Hyde Park. Six express packages had been sent on to her from Algonac, containing the wedding presents which she had wanted forwarded. These may have included the fine rich blue Chinese silk damask which her Papa had given her, and with which she planned to replace the gray silk curtains in the music room. But, for the rest, there would have been scant opportunity to make any changes in the South Parlor, with its mahogany sofa and chairs, or in the dining room, with the rose-crested chairs which had been saved from the fire at Mount Hope.

That efficient Scotswoman, Elspeth McEachern, who

had come in Rebecca Howland's time and whom the family always called Elespie, had quiet and spotless control over the household, continuing to do as she had done during the days of James Roosevelt's widowerhood. There was a cook to help her, and a housemaid. Since Harriet Wood had returned to Algonac after a few days, no personal maid for Mrs. Roosevelt is mentioned.

No entry in the Household Book can be traced to the fall of 1880; nor is that in the least surprising. It would be a really unnatural bride who would give much thought to recipes on her honeymoon. At Hyde Park there was too much to do in the open air, there were too many friends who called, too many informal dinner parties to attend, for her to grapple in stern earnest with this business of running a household, particularly when, for the moment, it seemed to run itself.

The Roosevelts had already been asked to dine at the home of the Maturin Livingstons in Staatsburgh—their first dinner party. Mr. Livingston was one of Ward McAllister's inner circle of New York society, and his daughter Ruth (called Teenie) became one of Mrs. Roosevelt's good friends. The gold and grandeur of the Livingston estate passed to Teenie after her marriage to Ogden Mills, and today is a state historical museum. The James Roosevelts' home was a simple country farmhouse compared to this over-ornamented elegance. But no Roosevelt or Delano had ever been over-awed by mere wealth, and they moved as naturally from Springwood to the Livingstons' at Staatsburgh as they did to plain, comfortable Rosedale.

Eleven days after the wedding Mrs. Roosevelt slipped down to Algonac to see them all, while her husband went on to New York on business. A week later her Papa and Mama left for the ten-o'clock train "to pay our *first* visit to Sallie and Mr. Roosevelt in her new home." The Delanos were met at the station and brought back to Springwood for breakfast.

After breakfast the party took a walk about the place, and then "Sallie rec'd visitors." In the afternoon the Delanos were driven up to Staatsburgh, where they all called on Mr. William B. Dinsmore at The Locusts, his fine new home on the river.

Papa and his son-in-law went on to New York the next day, and the ladies returned to Algonac; Mrs. Roosevelt left in time to meet her husband on the six-o'clock train.

Three days later the Roosevelts were again in Algonac, upon the occasion of another "grand torchlight procession" in Newburgh, which that Republican stronghold staged for the great cause of Garfield and Arthur. Mr. Roosevelt's sympathies being with Messrs. Hancock and English, the Democratic candidates for President and Vice-President, he was presumably not so enthusiastic as his Republican hosts. The bridal couple stayed until November 2, Election Day, and then went up river with Uncle Frank, Mr. Roosevelt to vote in Hyde Park and the latter in Barrytown. At Algonac, Papa, Uncle Ned, Phil, and two men on the place voted the Republican ticket, while all the Irishmen employed there gave their votes to the Democrats.

The light and colors fade from the hills in Dutchess and Orange Counties by the first of November, and the happy month at Hyde Park had drawn to a close. Mr. Roosevelt planed to stay only far enough into November to vote, and then take the next European sailing. On the fifth of that month the Delanos—Mama, Kassie, and Uncle Ned—came down to the Brevoort House in New York to bid their Sallie farewell. On the seventh of November the White Star liner *Germanic* got off from the dock and went to sea, as Papa, with the ineradicable touch of the old sailor, remarked, before the "strong fair wind that it is hoped may run the ship across to Queenstown."

For ten delightful months the Roosevelts wandered back and forth across Europe. They met Dora and Will Forbes in Italy, and through them met many of the Italian aristocracy. They both fell ill in Spain of some kind of fever, but with no serious results. In order to cheer her up, Mr. Roosevelt bought his wife a beautiful old Spanish lace mantilla, and got the landlord's daughter to show her how to wear it. Sallie, the *peineta* (a high tortoise-shell comb) banked with scarlet carnations, holding the mantilla at a becoming height above her dark hair, must have been entrancing.

The sights and sounds and smells of Europe were not the same, of course; but the society in the spring of 1881 was not so very different from that of New York, Newburgh, or Hyde Park. Maggie de Stuers and her husband and their children were there; the John Bigelows, whom Mrs. Roosevelt had so often visited at Malden on the Hudson, were there; and in April, Papa and Mama, Laura, Kassie, and Harriet Wood arrived in Paris with Dora and Will Forbes, and so the family reunion was complete, with the exception of Annie in far-off Shanghai, and Phil, whose health was now so delicate that he was unable to travel.

This was a holiday in true Delano fashion. Papa took a whole floor at the Hôtel du Rhin, and the entire family stayed together. With real unselfishness on the part of a honeymooning husband, James Roosevelt rented a brougham and spent many afternoons driving his wife and her young sisters about—to Versailles to see the fountains play, to the Bois, to the rue de Rivoli, to the Opéra Comique. There was something free, patriarchal, and thoroughly American in the way in which Warren Delano made of his large family one gay and pleasure-bent group, even to the extent of taking adjoining boxes at the opera. Mr. James Roosevelt, in his middle age, was learning how to adapt himself to a large and friendly family, and showed himself again to be the thoughtful, humorous man to whom nobody could refer except as "dear James."

After this great splurge of family activity in Paris—where, incidentally, they bought a Smyrna carpet for the house— the Roosevelts went to Belgium and then to Holland. Here they indulged in some serious shopping for the house at Hyde Park. They ordered silver and furniture, in particular the Dutch sideboard which still stands against the west wall in the dining room. This was made to order from panels selected in Amsterdam. They also bought a grandfather's clock in The Hague. This was placed in the front hall, almost directly opposite the front door, and is today one of the first objects one sees on entering the Roosevelt home. From Holland their journey led them to Germany, where Mrs. Roosevelt revisited Celle, scene of her German schooldays, and then they went to Switzerland, where another reunion took place, this time with Uncle Frank and Aunt Laura Delano.

By July the Roosevelts had arrived in England, for at that time James ordered a landau, a dogcart, and a victoria from Thorn, the carriage-maker at Norwich, and some fine English roses at Cheshunt. They had not planned to sail for home on the *Germanic* until September 1, so there was time for a visit to the Scottish Highlands, as well as time and opportunity to visit the many English friends who were eager to meet James Roosevelt's bride.

One of the most cordial invitations came from Sir Hugh and Lady Cholmeley of Easton, a fine Queen Anne house at Grantham. It is this Sir Hugh who at a later date was responsible for the "Soup of Green Pea Shoots" which appears in the Household Book. Another invitation took them to the home of Madame Schwabe, an Englishwoman married to a German, whom they had met in Naples. Here Mrs. James was introduced to an old acquaintance of her husband—a plain, dumpy little woman of sixty, in black taffeta, who answered to the name of Madame Goldschmidt. Music lovers will know that this was the great Swedish singer, Jenny Lind, whose voice had charmed all America many years before. For Sallie, who had spent so many hours studying singing, this was a rare occasion.

One is, of course, mercifully unaware of one's destiny and that of one's contemporaries. No one then living could have known what an extraordinary bridge between the past and the future was represented in this tall and slender young woman, whose serious dark eyes rested so fondly on her husband; she who was to become the mother of the most controversial president in America's history. Friend of many Victorian giants, product of the best in America's vigorous nineteenth-century society, she lived just beyond the day when the last vestige of that society was being swept away forever.

Mrs. Roosevelt was aware at this time that she was going to have a child and, for that reason among others, was anxious to be back in Hyde Park; although she felt that they had had such happy days all along and that James was wonderful in the way he took care of everything, and in his untiring and thoughtful devotion.

Sara Delano had always known her own mind; and in her youth had made decisions firmly and often wisely as circumstances required. In the course of her long and active life, she never showed better judgment as to what was right for her than when she married James Roosevelt. True, he was twenty-six years her senior; true, he had not quite the background in literature that she had acquired, or the deep interest in music, both as listener and performer, which was hers. He was, nevertheless, of the same American stock that had bred her. They were both convinced that as they had been fortunate enough to have been born to health, intelligence, and wealth, it was their duty to set an example before less favored men. Family ties wrapped both of them closely; family duties were paramount with both. The out-of-doors, good horses, good sleighing, good boating, good company, they both took as their heritage—pleasant concomitants to the business of leading upright, dutiful, honorable, and regulated lives.

Throughout their married life, James Roosevelt found in his wife a wholly congenial companion. Sara Roosevelt found in her husband her perfect complement, from whom she could not bear to be parted, whom she drove to the station when he needed to go away, and met upon his return, so that he should not be so long away from her.

Their honeymoon ended on September 10, and on their return to the United States they proceeded at once to Hyde Park, to find the house in "beautiful order," thanks to Elespie. They saw Helen and Rosy for a moment at their house —the Red House, which still stands next to Springwood and to which James and Rebecca Roosevelt's grandchildren still come. Then they went to have tea at Rosedale with Mother Roosevelt, John, Ellen, and the children. There was only one cloud on the horizon. Just before they sailed from England dear Uncle Ned succumbed in Bar Harbor to an acute stomach ailment which has the ring of appendicitis to modern ears. The death of this jolliest of childhood companions was hard to bear, so soon after losing Auntie.

Now the time had come for Mrs. Roosevelt actively to take over the management of her new home, and to make plans for her future. The water colors which she had bought abroad were hung, the Dutch furniture unpacked and found to have been rather damaged in shipping; the new carriages from England arrived, and she sat with Mrs. Rosy for an hour, watching her husband uncrate them. Elespie put down the Smyrna carpet which they had bought in Paris, and surely the blue silk curtains were hung at the windows of the music room.

But in the main, Christine Nilson, the cook engaged immediately after their arrival, seems to have been left largely to her own devices, since no recipes appear in the Household Book for this period. She should have been canning tomatoes, for Dutchess County produced a bumper crop that year.

Actually, the days seemed to drift along, filled with small pleasant happenings and no strenuous effort.

There was boating on the river in the mild fall weather, and drives; but the two pretty fillies, Minna and Brenda, sent over from Algonac by her Papa, did not, understandably, carry their new mistress over any woodland trails that autumn.

Nelly Blodgett came for a visit in October, and they took her over to see some oxen which Mr. Roosevelt was considering buying from a farmer in a nearby township. Rosy and his wife were blessed by the birth of a little girl, making Mr. Roosevelt a grandfather shortly before he became a father for the second time. The Roosevelts dined with the Archie Rogers, their neighbors to the north, who had lately built a mansion "after the English castle style," which would, when entirely completed, cost close to three hundred thousand dollars, as the writer of an article in the local paper opined. It was implied that since Mrs. Rogers enjoyed an income of a thousand dollars a day, this was only to be expected.

The Roosevelts lunched often with the Dinsmores; they went nearly every day to Rosedale, and dined with the Rosy Roosevelts almost every night.

Mr. Roosevelt's familiar figure was seen on the Hyde Park roads once more; his hat was lifted to men, women, and children; for, he said, he thought that children could best learn politeness if their elders were polite to them.

Dora and Will came to visit, and Kittie Crummie, the faithful dressmaker from Algonac, arrived to alter some of Mrs. Roosevelt's dresses.

Although the list for a layette in the Household Book is dated simply 1881, we can assume that serious consideration was given to the items Mrs. Low recommended at this time. Mrs. Abbot A. Low, the former Marian Ward, a close friend, was a daughter-in-law of the Lows who had rented Algonac during those difficult post-depression years when the Delano family was in China. This list contains only the essentials. No mention is made here of the christening dress, which was trimmed with rows and rows of find handmade tucks and Valenciennes lace; or of the wicker cradle, with its elaborate skirts of sheerest batiste, lace-edged, over pale blue silk; or of such other articles as Sara Roosevelt's first child might be expected to have had supplied for the adornment of infant and nursery.

Autumn slipped into winter, and shortly before Christmas, Philippe, the brother next to Mrs. Roosevelt, succumbed to the "grievous malady" which he had borne with wonderful patience, conscious, as his Papa put it, that for many years he had been living face to face with death. In the light of modern medical knowledge, the family's belief that this was epilepsy may have been erroneous. Even though he had been in failing health for so long, his death was still a hard blow for Sallie, coming so swiftly after Uncle Ned's.

But Christmas was celebrated at Hyde Park just the same, for the people on the place—"our people." The head farmer and the farmhands and the gardeners and Buckle, the excellent English coachman, and the stable boys, all got turkeys. A few small gifts were left at the Rogers', the Irvings', and the Livingstons', and Christmas dinner was eaten at Algonac—a good "turkey and plum pudding dinner."

Then the winter began in earnest. The newspapers ran articles on how to treat chilblains; the Poughkeepsie *Daily Eagle* averred that a turnip poultice was good, the feet to be bathed in the water in which turnips had been boiled. Skating parks were for the first time illuminated at night with electric lights.

The Poughkeepsie Ice Yacht Club, John A. Roosevelt Commodore, challenged the New Hamburg Ice Yacht Club for the championship flag of America. Brother John had had built for him the largest iceboat in the world, the *Icicle,* today to be seen in the Franklin D. Roosevelt Library. She had wire rigging, the best duck sails, nickel-plated blocking, velvet-upholstered cockpit, a polished hardwood hull, and steel runners for both hard and soft ice. Brother John could speed eighty miles an hour with her when the wind was right, and ice yachting had become very popular, dangerous sport though it was, all up and down the Hudson.

From the upstairs windows, Mrs. Roosevelt could watch the Poughkeepsie Ice Yacht Club's blue regatta flag flash past as the *Icicle* tore before the wind, Aaron Innis's *Haze* close behind her.

It grew cold and colder, and Mrs. Roosevelt kept to the house, trying some songs in the music room, arranging her "dear flowers" from the greenhouses, dining on a little pig which Papa had sent over, and reading aloud with her husband. When reading palled, for Mr. Roosevelt did not share the Algonac passion for reading aloud, there was bezique and piano practice and sewing to fill in the long hours of waiting, for the baby was expected within the month.

Ice was cut and the icehouses all filled—a matter of great

importance to the families living on the Hudson. It is said
that as much as a million tons of ice were stored in the icehouses along the river. In the years when ice was poor,
people were lucky if they could buy any in midsummer, and
so every able-bodied man who could drive a team and wield
an ice saw got out, as soon as the ice was eight inches thick,
and helped haul ice for dear life.

Besides the icehouses, the Roosevelt home had an ice
pantry, running through what was in later years the butler's
pantry, so that the butler and serving personnel had to go
out into the hall and enter the dining room by a hall door.
This was an awkward arrangement, particularly if there
were many guests, but the great convenience of having a
cold room which could be filled with ice from outside the
house more than made up for the extra steps from the kitchen
to the dining room.

The trained nurse, Mrs. Lee, who had been engaged for
the great event at twenty dollars a week, arrived on January 14. However, Mrs. Roosevelt was feeling perfectly well.
The snow was now ideal for sleighing, so she continued to
drive out in the small Russian sleigh with her husband. He
had bought this charming vehicle for fifteen dollars at an
auction in Paris in 1872. It had been designed for Alexander II of Russia and given by him to Napoleon III of
France. It was lined with red velvet and carpeted with
flowered Brussels, and the elegance of the curvings and carvings made it unique along the Albany Post Road.

Sunday, January 29, 1882, was one of those cold, dis-
agreeable, blustery days which sends the whole world
shivering to the fireside. The wind was sharp and bitter,
dropping the mercury to fifteen degrees above zero at Hyde
Park, and making the sidewalks so slippery that walking
in Poughkeepsie was very difficult. At seven-thirty on the
evening of that day, the Roosevelts realized that the time

of waiting was over. Mr. Roosevelt was up and down all night, and at six o'clock the morning of the thirtieth he called the nurse, Mrs. Lee. At seven the doctor was sent for.

Monday, January 30, although cold, dawned bright and clear, and by half-past nine in the morning Dr. Edward H. Parker had made his way up the Albany Post Road to Springwood. This physician and surgeon was well known in medical circles. He had been, in 1862, President of the New York Medical Society, and had served with distinction as a volunteer surgeon in the field during the Civil War. He was locally known "for his skillful practice among a large private clientele," and Dutchess County was considered fortunate to have living within its borders a medical practitioner of such pre-eminence. In addition, the doctor was personally "refined, cultivated, suave, very liberal and sympathetic." Mr. Roosevelt was entirely confident that Dr. Parker could bring the best obstetrical knowledge and technique to the problem which now confronted him at Springwood.

By noon a telegram had reached Algonac, greeting Mrs. Delano as she came back from a drive to Newburgh in the big sleigh. She caught the four-o'clock train to Hyde Park and was met at the station at seven P.M. by an anxious son-in-law. At eight o'clock the doctor resorted to chloroform. Forty-five minutes later Sara Roosevelt bore a "splendid large boy" weighing ten pounds, in the double bed which today can be seen in the front bedroom of the house at Hyde Park.

There is in the Franklin D. Roosevelt Library the note which Mr. Roosevelt scratched off on a telegraph blank—the first piece of paper that came to hand—telling the family at Rosedale of this satisfactory climax. It is addressed to "Dear Ellen" (his sister-in-law), and reads: "I have only a moment before Dr. Parker leaves to write you that Sallie has a bouncing boy. Poor child, she has had a very hard time. The boy was born at 9 P.M. [sic] and Dr. P. has been here since this A.M. 9:30. Sallie sends her love her mother is with her." The doctor delivered this on his way back to Poughkeepsie, late the same evening.

This experienced physician, then a gentleman nearing sixty years of age, had had a long and tiring day, and must have felt some degree of satisfaction that the baby he had ushered into the world in the James Roosevelt home was so large and healthy. His bill for this service amounted to fifty dollars, and the eight visits following were listed at three dollars each. Together with his fee for calls previous to the baby's birth, his total reimbursement for this significant medical service was a hundred dollars. According to the best practice of the period, he kept Mrs. Roosevelt confined to her room for nearly four weeks, and it was not until February 26 that she reappeared at the dinner table. She was, of course, nursing the baby, who continued to thrive, and who was, in the Delano tradition, referred to simply as "Baby"or "darling Baby."

The prescriptions for croup and diarrhea and Mrs. Lee's remedy for thrush were noted in the Household Book at this time by Baby's apprehensive mother.

Mr. Roosevelt went in search of a nurse for this lusty infant, and engaged an Englishwoman for eighteen dollars a month. She was not satisfactory, so then sister Dora interviewed and engaged Helen McRorie, "a good experienced woman and very gentle." This was the "Ellen" to whom the whole family became so devoted, but who was called "Mamie" by her young charge as soon as he was able to speak. Ellen did not arrive in time for the christening, which took place on March 20, 1882, but "Baby was quite good and lovely" without her. He was named Franklin Delano (after Uncle Frank). His godfathers were Elliott Roosevelt, brother of Theodore Roosevelt, Jr., and Dora's husband, Will

Forbes. The latter was unfortunately suffering from a bad attack of gout and could not attend, so "dear James" stood proxy for him. Nelly Blodgett was godmother. Kassie, Mama and Papa Delano, Ellen Roosevelt, and Captain and Mrs. Randolph were present to watch Dr. Cady, Rector of St. James, receive this rosy child into the fellowship of Christ. After the ceremony a simple lunch was served at Springwood.

There had, of course, been many guests in the Roosevelt home after the return from Europe, and before the baby was born. But, as was natural, it was not until Mrs. Roosevelt was fully recovered and a competent nurse had been engaged that the household was organized on permanent principles. There were now frequent visitors in the guest rooms. The meals took on more formal character than the simple lunches and dinners served to Mr. and Mrs. Roosevelt between September 1881 and April 1882. A family luncheon would consist of soup, fish, and chicken, with perhaps rice pudding for dessert. A dinner for Rosy and his wife or the Rosedale family might offer soup (of which Mrs. Roosevelt was always very fond), fish and meat, vegetables, and dessert. There were usually roast beef and Yorkshire pudding for Sundays, and turkey with squash and mince pie for holidays.

James Roosevelt's granddaughter Helen (Mrs. Theodore Douglas Robinson) remembers that her grandfather always carved the turkey, and that his wife, whom she called Aunt Sallie, always served soup out of a large soup tureen, ladling it out herself. It is an early matriarchal touch. One notes that there are seven recipes for soup in the Household Book.

With a sizable cold pantry (approximately ten feet by six), it was possible to keep many home-grown farm delicacies fresh for several days, and Christine, the cook, should have been able to turn out delicious meals. There was a coal-

and-wood-burning range in the kitchen, with a hot-water boiler beside it, and the pots and pans were suspended from a rack hanging over a long worktable. There was one sink in the kitchen and another in the butler's pantry, although the water pumped from springs by a combination of wind-mill, water-tank, and hydraulic ram was not entirely inex-haustible. The servants' bath in the service wing, and the one bathroom for the main house, were carefully main-tained on the "two inches of water only in the tub" schedule during extended dry spells.

That Mrs. Roosevelt was now gathering the household reins more tightly into her own hands is evidenced by the fact that entries in the Household Book begin again, after a lapse of two years, following recipes copied from her sister-in-law, Mrs. Warren Delano III, during a visit to Mount Savage in the fall of 1880, just before Sallie's own marriage. The recipe for strawberry preserves, as well as the currant jelly recipe, was noted during the berry season, and one may conclude that the strawberry recipe was given to Mrs. James Roosevelt by her mother-in-law, Mrs. Dr. Isaac, at the same time that the universal "pint of juice, pound of sugar" formula for currant jelly was handed on.

All during the summer following Baby Franklin's birth, there was shuttling and traveling up and down the Post Road and up and down the river—to Algonac, to Steen Valetje, to Rhinebeck, to meet the Grand Duke Alexander at the William Astors', to Rosedale, and to the Red House. There was a month in town with Will and Dora Forbes—a jaunt on which Baby went along. This was followed by his first summer pilgrimage, made by all good Delanos, to Fair-haven.

Harriet Wood, now the mainstay at Algonac, since Kassie had married Mr. C. A. Robbins in April, furnished the "Very strong Chicken & Beef Tea for an invalid," during one of the Algonac visits that first year of Franklin's life, together with recipes for mushroom catsup and pickled onions. Poor Harriet Wood! It had been her lot to nurse three fatal illnesses—Nannie, Auntie, and Phil—since she had come to Algonac permanently in the early winter of 1880. No wonder she knew so many recipes suitable for invalids.

In the fall of 1882 Baby went to his first party, at the Henry Rogerses', and was so intent on joining the other children's dancing that his mother could hardly hold him. For his first Christmas there was a tree trimmed for him and "all the people on the place," and Christmas dinner at Algonac; and just before his first birthday, he was taken to New York for a few months, to the house rented furnished at 31 West Forty-ninth Street.

It was here that Baby had a bad fall on a tin toy and cut his little nose, while his mother was out. It bled terribly, and his father was frightened to death, but the doctor assured them the wound would heal without a scar—which it did.

The summer of 1883 found the Roosevelts with Baby and Ellen at Campobello, a small island seventy miles northeast of Mount Desert, Maine. They had decided on that vacation spot in order that Mr. Roosevelt might get in some good sailing. They stayed at the Tyn y Coed (House in the Woods), an inn with comfortable rooms and open fires, where many of their friends were also guests, among them the Russell Sturgises of Boston and Mr. and Mrs. James Lawrence of Groton.

Together with his brother, Mr. Lawrence had recently donated approximately one hundred acres of land in that small Massachusetts village for a boys' preparatory school, which was to be run by Endicott Peabody, a recent graduate of the Episcopal Theological School in Cambridge. At the time of this meeting with the Lawrences in Campobello, Baby Franklin's name was put down on the waiting list of this school, although it was not yet in operation. The Lawrences lived near the as yet uncompleted school buildings, and Mrs. Roosevelt took comfort in the thought that in the far-off days when the toddling little boy should have to leave her he would be close to such good friends. The Roosevelts had a kettle and a tea-caddy in their rooms that summer, and possibly a chafing dish, so that they could entertain friends for tea. On one of these occasions they tasted Mrs. Lawrence's Welsh rarebit and found it good enough to add to the Household Book.

This summer outing proved such a success that before they left Campobello, Mr. and Mrs. Roosevelt bought four acres of land on the sea, and made arrangements to have a cottage built for them in time for occupancy the following summer.

The family did not move in as planned, however, for the fall of 1884 found them in Europe (with Baby Franklin, Elespie, and Ellen). Mr. Roosevelt, now past the middle fifties, felt the European water cures to be very helpful and relaxing, and wished to go to Bad Kissingen. While Mrs. Roosevelt accompanied him to this Bavarian village, the baby, with his two faithful nurses, was left behind in Tunbridge Wells, England. The recipe for barley broth is a memento of this German visit.

The recipes for Devonshire cream, Devonshire pudding, and ginger pudding stem from this same European sojourn. After leaving Bad Kissingen, the Roosevelts returned to spend December 1884, and January, February, and March 1885, in St. Leonard's-on-Sea and Tunbridge Wells; they did not return to Hyde Park until April 1885. The Mrs. Bennett who so kindly supplied the recipe for Devonshire cream—that delicious English specialty—has not been identified. The Bessie mentioned in these recipes may have been the cook at Tunbridge Wells, which would indicate that the

Roosevelts had taken a furnished villa in that beautifully sit-
uated Kentish spa, since prolonged hotel life with an active
child of three might easily undo all the good effects of the
sulphur baths and Rakoczy Well at Kissingen. Tunbridge
Wells was a wonderfully healthy spot, with its wooded
walks and parks. Ellen and Elespie surely took Baby Franklin to Rusthall Common to climb upon that strange mass of
sandstone called Toad Rock, or wandered with him past the
Queen Anne houses, relics of a day when Tunbridge Wells
did not yield even to Bath as a health resort for fashionable
society.

Before the Roosevelts left for home, they visited their old
friends, Sir Hugh and Lady Cholmeley, at Easton again—
acquiring the recipe for "Soup of Green Pea Shoots"—and
made a round of great English country houses including
Belvoir Castle, the Duke of Rutland's seat. Mr. Roosevelt
rode to hounds with the Belvoir Hunt, Mrs. Roosevelt and
the gouty old Duke following in a carriage.

By April they wanted to be back in the house at Hyde
Park, and booked passage on the *Germanic*. There was a
dreadful storm at sea, and the *Germanic* was so badly damaged by the exceedingly heavy waves that at the request of
many aboard, Mr. Roosevelt among them, the captain put
back to Liverpool to transfer his passengers to the *Adriatic*.

Many liners have passed through many storms, and as
long as there is a happy ending, such marine adventures
are apt to be forgotten on dry land. Mrs. Roosevelt described
this experience to Mrs. Kleeman, who reports it in her book
Gracious Lady. It is the epitome of Delano character.

"On Easter Sunday morning," she related, "there was a
dreadful storm, and James, after breakfasting with the Captain, came back to tell me that I couldn't go on deck. As
he talked the ship seemed suddenly to drop into a trough
in the sea and everything became dark. I said,

" 'We seem to be going down.'

" 'It does look like it,' he replied.

"Though I did not want him to leave us, he went out in search of information.

"After what seemed a long time, he returned and said that the Captain had disappeared and could not be found. Several boats were lost, and a bulk-head in the reading room above our cabin had been broken. We could already hear the water rushing over our heads. Almost immediately it began to come into our cabin.

"I never get frightened and I was not then.

"But when the water was high enough to touch the bottom of a fur coat that was hanging by my berth, I took it and wrapped it around the baby, saying to my husband,

" 'Poor little boy, if he must go down, he is going down warm.' "

The entry in the Household Book for May 5, 1885, picks up the thread of Sara Roosevelt's Hudson Valley life again. There were the walks and the drives and the boating on the river and the frequent trips to Algonac—more frequent now, for another tragedy had broken over the Delanos' heads just the year before. The news of this awful catastrophe was given to the Roosevelts over the telephone newly installed at Hyde Park.

Annie and Fred Hitch had come home from Shanghai in July, reaching Algonac on a Saturday afternoon. The next morning the family was assembled on the lawn, waiting for Laura to finish dressing, when there was an explosion as of a pistol, followed by an agonizing shriek. Laura flashed down the stairway, a cloud of fiery flame, out through the hall into the open air. Fred Hitch, standing in the hall, could not stop her, but, seizing a rug, he dashed after her and managed to suppress the flames. Her negligee had caught in the alcohol lamp which she was using to heat her curling irons and it exploded and burned her so frightfully that she died early the next morning. This was a hard blow for Warren and Catherine Delano, and they did indeed feel that their hearts were broken and they could not be comforted. Of the eleven children born to them, only six were left.

Dora, Annie, Sallie, and Kassie—all the girls were married. Warren III was married too, and only Fred, at the age of twenty-five was still a bachelor. Mama and Papa Delano were now more alone than they had been for forty years, so Annie and Fred Hitch, returning no more to the Orient, quartered permanently at Algonac, to use old Mr. Delano's language. Mrs. Hitch, the always capable sister Annie, took up the reins of the household management again, and it was to her that the family turned with problems large and small, as they had done in the days before her marriage.

After six months abroad, Mrs. Roosevelt needed to be introduced to the latest culinary news, which would explain the reference to Miss Parloa. Miss Maria Parloa, principal of the School of Cooking in Boston, was the forerunner of Fannie Farmer; in fact, Miss Farmer had studied at her school and assisted the Director before she opened her own School of Cookery. Miss Parloa's *New Cook Book*, published in 1884, was the final authority on culinary matters, to be found in every well-run kitchen.

The recipe for Oyster Toast calls for an accolade to Mr. Charlesworth, if he could be identified. The admonition to "eat it in solemn silence and wash down with a glass of brown sherry or cherry brandy" sounds as if it were he, and not Mrs. Hitch or Mrs. Roosevelt, speaking. Cooking was not a joking matter at Springwood, and the mistress of the house, giving instructions to the cook, reading aloud to her such recipes from the Household Book as were to be prepared, would not have been jocular about it.

After two months at Hyde Park, the Roosevelts were at last ready to inspect the new cottage at Campobello, which had been ready for them for a year. There was furniture bought in London to be installed, and Baby and Ellen to be settled. Furthermore, there was an opportunity for some fine sailing with Dr. Russell Sturgis of Boston, with whom Mr. Roosevelt had bought a sailboat. Dr. and Mrs. Sturgis were friends of long standing—descendants of the Sturgis family of Boston who had had business dealings with Warren Delano II in the China trade half a century before. While the men sailed, Mrs. Roosevelt and Mrs. Sturgis must have talked over household matters, for the recipes for curry and curry powder were supplied by the latter—a fine Oriental touch to a family friendship originally begun in the Far East.

The cottage at Campobello, more properly described as a fairly large, rambling house, was far from elaborate, finished and furnished in the simplest seaside resort fashion, but it could accommodate so many guests that a procession of the Roosevelt friends moored off the landing and came and went across the wide verandas.

This was an era when only well-to-do people traveled for pleasure—by boat, by train, by carriage. Today the automobile has put this possibility of motion within the means of nearly everyone, and caused a great deal of talk about "mobile America." In the eighties those who could afford to travel apparently never stayed home.

From the moment of Franklin's birth, it was assumed by his parents that their son would in no important way interfere with the kind of life which both of them enjoyed— this life of travel; self-gratification, if you will; this urbane kind of existence, in which the wealthy could indulge to their hearts' content. No journeys were given up because of Baby, no sacrifices of time or purpose were made because of him. He became a youthfully pleasant adjunct of their lives, molded to their demands, his education and his pleasures determined by the traveling schedule of his parents. This pattern was by no means unique. At that period, and among their friends, it was accepted as quite normal that the Roosevelts should do this. Less affluent families might move to or away from certain localities solely for the sake of their children; might affiliate themselves with certain social groups or refrain from doing so for the same reason; might scrimp and save and deny themselves in order to afford better educations for their sons. It was not necessary for the Roosevelts to be influenced by such considerations; nor did they think of any other kind of life for their child than the one which their own mature tastes and preferences forced upon him. People of means in those days were much more inclined, as compared with modern parents in any financial category, to lay down a pretty complete blueprint for the lives of their children, much of it predicated upon their own conveniences and recreations.

As soon, then, as Franklin was old enough to be taken along with a nurse—or to be left at Algonac, if his parents were bound for such unhealthful spots as Mexico—Mr. and Mrs. James Roosevelt were constantly on the move. They spent several months of each winter on Forty-ninth Street in New York, and after 1888 at the Hotel Renaissance on West Forty-third Street, where they kept a small apartment. They usually went to Europe in the spring and to Campobello in the summer, and made many long railroad journeys across the United States during the months between these major hegiras. As a director of the Delaware and Hudson Railroad, Mr. Roosevelt had at his disposal for such

journeys the railroad's private car, the *Monon,* staffed by
William Yapp, Negro cook and porter. His recipe for egg
bread appears in the Household Book, and if it is a fair
sample of the meals he served the Roosevelts, travel aboard
the *Monon* must have been a very pleasant way to get about.

Ensconced in the *Monon's* sitting room and bedrooms, the
Roosevelts went to Bar Harbor, to Portland, to Montreal, to
Mexico—over most of the routes of the Louisville, New Albany and Chicago Railroad, of which Mr. Roosevelt was
president, as well as over the tracks of the numerous small
holdings of the Delaware and Hudson.

Mr. Roosevelt's railroad interests, as well as the family
pleasure trips, now took him frequently away from Hyde
Park. The sight of this side-whiskered gentleman was more
and more uncommon, riding down to Hyde Park post office
for the mail, walking to Hyde Park village for a morning's
exercise, speaking to his friends and neighbors on the way,
calling at the Hudson River State Hospital, silk-hatted as
befitted a manager, dignified and pleasant.

One saw Mrs. Roosevelt even more rarely—that tall dark
woman, with a touch of imperiousness already marked in
the carriage of her head and in the direct, serious look of
her brown eyes. The parishioners of St. James Episcopal
Church, of which Mr. Roosevelt had been a warden and a
vestryman for more than forty years, might count on seeing
him, his wife and son in the small Victorian church on Sunday, rain or shine, when the family was in Hyde Park; but
travelers up or down the Albany Post Road could no longer
catch a glimpse of the squire, sitting in his sulky, exercising
his trotters in the field to the southeast of his home. Gloster,
his famous trotter, the first to do the mile under 2:20, had
long ago been sold. Trotting races were no longer a gentleman's sport, and the last of the stable, Doolittle, became Mr.
Roosevelt's saddle horse, while a mare named Josie was, as

Franklin D. Roosevelt recalled, the driving horse for years.

There was less time for rowing on the river and for walk-ing or driving out in the woodland paths about Springwood. With the death of Mrs. Dr. Isaac Roosevelt, James' gentle mother, in 1886, the reasons for taking the river or the Post Road to Rosedale no longer had such urgency. This patient wife and intelligent, unselfish mother lived to be seventy-seven years of age; she left to her sons the heritage of the staunch Aspinwall blood, and a pattern for her son James' wife to follow, in the words written to Dr. Isaac so long ago: "My dear husband, I am still willing to abide by your de-cision for then I shall be perfectly satisfied for *you* will then be happy."

Now there were the races at Jerome Park, to which they went in Rosy's coach. There was the opera, seen from the box of Mr. James A. Roosevelt, brother of Theodore Roosevelt, Sr.; he was one of the founders of the Metropolitan. There were recitals by Paderewski, and parties for him afterward at Nelly Blodgett's, and attendance at Ward McAllister's as-tonishing Patriarchs' Balls held on Monday evening between New Year's and Lent to work society up to the real event of the season, Mrs. Astor's ball.

The Roosevelts, in town for the winter, would perhaps go to the opera first, and then at a fashionably late hour take a carriage down to Delmonico's at Twenty-sixth Street and Fifth Avenue, to look in on the Patriarchs and watch a happy debutante lead the cotillion. The florists in those days must have led a blissful life. For a Patriarchs' Ball the corridors were bordered with plants and orchids, the chan-deliers in the ballroom were hung with pink roses, and the orchestras played on rose-garlanded balconies. The supper menu was always overlavish, indigestible, and written en-tirely in French: *Salade de Crabes Nonpareil, Mayonnaise de Poulet, Terrapène à la Trenton, Filet de Boeuf, Sauce*

Béarnaise Tomatée, Bavarois aux Fraises; and almost humbly at the bottom of the menu, "Champagne, Special Cuvée A. and Apollinaris."

The home and the farm did not suffer during these absences. Irving, the farmer, was a good man and had been with Mr. Roosevelt so long that he knew just how things should be done. He kept a steady stream of fresh produce from the three-hundred-and-ninety-acre tract pouring into the big cold pantry at Springwood. In the winter, when the family was in New York, farm products were sent down to them; in summer, when they were at Campobello, baskets of fruits and vegetables continued to flow in cornucopial abundance from the Roosevelt farm. This now included a large section of land across the Post Road from the house, on which the farm barns had been built, and where farm operations were farther removed from the residence.

In 1887 Allan, the butler, left—the one who had greeted Mrs. Roosevelt on her return from her European honeymoon —and a one-eyed character named Charles Anderson came to take his place. There are those who remember what an electric effect his glass eye had on small children, but he was a good servant for all that, and stayed ten years. Thereafter he went to Mrs. Roosevelt's brother, Warren III, who had inherited Steen Valetje from Uncle Franklin, and remained with the Delano family for forty-two years more.

Elespie, increasingly deaf, was still the pivot around which the household swung. She and Anderson, a cook, a maid, and a laundress kept the establishment going; so that after every journey Mrs. Roosevelt could note: "Got home and found everything in good order." Elespie also moved with the family when they went to New York, or when, as in the winter of 1887, they rented a house on K Street in Washington. The Washington experience was socially delightful, for the Roosevelts met all sorts of important people, including, of course, President Cleveland, who was an old friend of Mr. Roosevelt. It is more than a rumor, it is actually a fact, that President Cleveland did his best to persuade James Roosevelt to accept a diplomatic post, but that the Hudson Valley Democrat quietly and absolutely refused. His son, Rosy Roosevelt, might make a career of diplomacy, as indeed he did, but there was something rockbound and sturdy in the father which tied him to the country and the soil, in spite of the seeming restlessness which drove him and his wife and child away from Hyde Park every two or three months during this decade.

Mr. Roosevelt's recipe for egg-nog was not necessarily entered in the Household Book during the Washington winter. (That "suspicion of nutmeg" sounds like him; a woman would have said, "Dust lightly with nutmeg.") But egg-nog is a winter drink—and an invalid's drink, too, for that matter—and would match well with Miss Riggs' prescription for a cough. Miss Riggs may have been a friend, or a trained nurse, particularly in view of the fact that Mama Delano, who had come to visit, had quite a cold for some days, which, coming so soon after an attack of typhoid fever, caused her family considerable worry.

As for sewer gas, one can only hope that this peppermint test did not need to be applied at Springwood but in the rented Washington house, which was, unfortunately, far from clean when the Roosevelts moved in. A later test at Hyde Park showed only one or two *slight* leaks.

By 1888 Franklin was graduated from the loving Ellen to the care of a German governess, and the family were longer at Hyde Park than usual. They were there for the winter and spring of that year, as well as for the strawberry season, as Mrs. Archie Rogers' recipe for preserved strawberries indicates.

Mrs. Roosevelt began about this time to keep a scrap-

book, in which she pasted newspaper clippings of interest
(with no reference to the newspaper in which they appeared, unfortunately), and such a clipping, dated 1888,
gives a contemporary account of Hyde Park as it appeared
to a rhapsodic reporter. "The Kirchner place," he wrote, "is
now owned by James Roosevelt. Then comes the house of
J. R. Roosevelt, who wedded a daughter of William Astor,
and who has been recently appointed to the post of secretary
of the legation at Vienna. Then the home of James Roosevelt, who dwells there in quiet happiness with his wife,
a most estimable lady celebrated both in Europe and America for her loveliness and goodness. Then the residence of
Thomas Newbold, ex-senator from this district and president of the State Board of Health, and prominent among
the well-known Democrats of this state.

"We are now approaching the cozy little village of Hyde
Park, and the grand residence of Archie Rogers,—the
stables cost $46,000 and the coachman's house $18,000. Thus
in a short time we have travelled over possibly the most
beautiful drive in America. In winter trotters sweep over it
and lovely women enjoy the winter scenes along it. In summer stately trees shelter the road admitting an occasional
gleam of sunshine through the deepened shade, while the
youth, wealth and beauty of the city seek refreshment and
entertainment in its charming scenery."

A second clipping, for October 1888, mentions the third
run for the season of the Dutchess County Hunt, which took
place at W. P. Rogers'. The fox, it stated, ran over James
Roosevelt's broad acres, through a piece of woods, over the
hills and lowlands, bringing up on the hill east of John
Roosevelt's home. "There were many jumps along the run,
and now and then the people in the carriages on the Hyde
Park Road had a full view of the hounds and riders, making the scene exciting and enjoyable."

Hunt breakfasts were served at Springwood upon such occasions to as many as forty guests. The invaluable Miss Parloa suggests that oatmeal or hominy should always be served at breakfast, and gives a possible menu, consisting of fruit, oatmeal and cream, baked potatoes, mutton chops, rye muffins, hominy griddle-cakes, coffee, tea, or chocolate. There is no mention of the "stirrup cup," but a hunt breakfast patterned after the English manner would seem incredible without it.

It is significant that among the recipes noted during this period there appears another invalid delicacy, the wine whey. Mr. Roosevelt's health was not exactly a matter for concern, but the heart condition which had sent him to Bad Kissingen now made trips to European resorts or "cures" a yearly occurrence.

In 1889 the Roosevelts left Hyde Park for Europe in the summer, even though Franklin was not well at the time of their departure. The boy developed typhoid on the ship, and his condition gave his parents the greatest anxiety. Upon arriving at Liverpool, the seven-year-old was sent to the Royal Infirmary, where he eventually made a good recovery; but because of his condition, as well as Mr. Roosevelt's, the family left England in October, not for home but for Pau in the Basses-Pyrénées, where the mild climate would be good for both father and son. Mrs. Roosevelt rented an apartment and found satisfactory domestics—a butler named Auguste, at a hundred francs a month, a housemaid at thirty francs a month, and a cook at seventy francs.

It was this culinary artiste who contributed the recipe for Mont Blanc, a favorite French dessert.

Once in Pau, Franklin was well enough to ride for two hours every morning with his father, the latter on a large horse with the appropriate Gallic name of Zizi, the boy on a small pony equally well-named Coquette.

Since the Roosevelts did not choose to send their son to
school, but kept him with them, first under the instruction
of German and Swiss governesses, and later under tutors, it
followed that he was far more in the company of his parents than were most small children. The admirable Mlle. San-
doz came to them upon their return from Pau, and stayed for
more than three years.

His father had the boy constantly with him when he was
not on business trips, and together they superintended the
operation of the farm, inspected the greenhouses, rowed on
the river, and sailed at Campobello. It was an odd companionship, in a way, between a white-whiskered elderly man
and the small boy—a man, moreover, whose dignity of bearing and apparent unbendingness made him seem to his
Hyde Park neighbors a gentleman "who would stand no
nonsense." Yet there were jokes between them and a good
deal of laughter—more, it might be surmised, than burst
out in the presence of Sara Roosevelt. Even if Mr. Roosevelt would stand no nonsense, he is also remembered as a
man who was "jokey," with a fondness for that particular
kind of practical joke at which his son became a past
master.

Rosy's daughter Helen, who had strong tomboy preferences, according to her own testimony, and who played with
Franklin and her brother Taddy more frequently than she
did with little girls, remembers that her grandfather nearly
broke her heart one Christmas by giving her a great big doll
—a plaything she abhorred. The child was so shocked and
disappointed that she burst out crying, and her tender-hearted
grandfather, appalled at the way his joke had miscarried,
took her at once into the hall, where she found her real
present, a wonderful toboggan.

Franklin Roosevelt himself remembered how he used
to go out with his father on the numerous visits to the

schoolhouse or to the Hudson River State Hospital, ostensibly to hold the horses while his father was at board meetings.

"I remember," he told the graduating class of nurses at that institution in 1937, "one of the few times I ever saw my father thoroughly upset. He came back into the carriage to drive home, and he was quite silent. I knew he wanted me to say something, and so I said, 'What happened?'"

"'Well,' he said, 'I had the most terrible time because we were going though one of the wards and there was a perfectly dear sweet old lady in the ward, but as soon as she caught sight of me, she jumped out of her chair and said, "Why, Albert, don't you remember your Vicky?"

"'She insisted that she was Queen Victoria, and I was the Prince Consort!'"

The reminiscences of William R. Wright, for many years a superintendent at Hudson River State Hospital, who began work there as a messenger boy for his father, the watchman, shed further light on the Roosevelt propensity for joking.

"My father always told me to look out for Mr. James Roosevelt when he came," Mr. Wright would relate, and then add dryly, "I was to jump out, hold the horses or tie them up, particularly if that young scamp Franklin was along. He used to like to play practical jokes—hiding on the grounds and talking to the patients, and things like that."

The summer that Franklin was nine Mr. Roosevelt put his new forty-five foot yacht with an auxiliary motor in the water at Campobello. The *Half Moon* carried sail, of course, but her naphtha engine would speed her along at a rate of six and a half miles an hour for three hundred miles, and made cruising in her quartered-oak cabins a fine luxury. James Roosevelt taught his son to sail, and spent hours with

him on the waters off the coast of Maine. Mrs. Roosevelt
went along too, but seems occasionally to have injected a
Delano and rather feminine touch by reading aloud when
the wind died down.

To the present generation it is astonishing that a man
long past middle age, who visited spas in search of more
robust health, should at the same time be able to ride, to
hunt, to go sailing, and to keep many diversified business affairs firmly in hand. For instance, James Roosevelt was past
sixty when he became engaged in the organization of a
Land and River Improvement Company in Superior, Wisconsin. He bought Superior real estate in a large way, purchasing one office building for $125,000 and building a
block of dwellings called the Roosevelt Terrace at a cost of
$80,000. Mr. Roosevelt had experience in the Middle West
as a member of the Board of Directors of the First National
Bank in Superior, and as president of the West Superior
Iron and Steel Company, a field of business into which
his association with railroads and transportation systems
had naturally led him. There were those who said he saw
in Superior another Chicago—a vision doomed to vanish, for
in 1893 one of the recurrent depressions caused business
gradually to dwindle and shrink away. Although opinion
in Superior always considered Mr. Roosevelt one of the
wealthiest men in the East, which he was not by a long way,
it also maintained that he had lost considerable money in
his Wisconsin transactions, which he probably did.

In 1893 the Roosevelts visited the World's Fair in Chicago, not once but several times, traveling in the faithful
Monon. Mr. Roosevelt had been appointed an alternate com-
missioner to the Fair, representing the State of New York.
Mr. Chauncey Depew was chairman of the New York
Commission, appointed by President Harrison, and, being
exceptionally vigorous, had no need of an alternate. Mr.

Depew's address at a complimentary dinner given by the National Commissioners at Delmonico's, to which Mr. Roosevelt was invited, was resonantly eloquent, but not strictly veracious. He declared that the great Columbian Exposition would start an era of much prosperity, that farm mortgages would be paid off, new enterprises started, old railroads extended, new ones constructed; everybody would be richer and in accord with the temper and spirit of the American people; credit would be strained to the utmost to realize the largest returns from these phenomenal opportunities.

Apparently it had turned out to be not quite as simple as that for the entrepreneurs in the Land & River Improvement Company, as James Roosevelt could testify. Riches did not flood Superior as a result of the Columbian Exposition. But the Roosevelts did enjoy the great show Chicago was putting on. They took Edmund Rogers and Franklin along for one visit, during which the small boys were so enthralled with the Indians who could pick up pennies by flicking whips at them that this art was faithfully practiced at Hyde Park for some time after their return.

There is a story to the effect that Franklin, when he accompanied his parents on one of his father's many visits to Superior, came very near drowning. They were attending the launching of a whaleback ore boat. As the ship hit the water, a large wave caused by the splash rolled over a pier on which Franklin was standing, and he was swept into the bay. Presumably he was rescued!

In 1894 Mr. Roosevelt was made vice-president of the Delaware and Hudson Railroad, and then president of the Champlain Transportation Company, which ran paddle-wheel streamers on the Adirondack lakes. The peripatetic Roosevelts, after a decade of shuttling from continent to continent and country to city, seemed now to be settling into a routine which permitted Mr. Roosevelt to take on more

rather than to resign from business and civic duties. Although he had been a member of the school board in Hyde
Park since 1881, and elected president at that time, his attendance at meetings had of necessity been most irregular.
In the nineties he found time to preside once more, and
the minutes of the board note "Mr. James Roosevelt in the
chair," with regularity. It was not an onerous office, as the
board met chiefly to approve bills. Mr. Thomas W. Rider
constituted a committee of one to visit the school once a
month, and since he always reported that everything was
in perfect order, there was little action. The board's func-
tion was mostly to deal with money matters, for instance,
to cut the salary of the truant officer from seven and a half
dollars a month to five dollars a month, with an accompany-
ing change in title to "constable"; to raise the pay of Mrs.
Lane, a remarkable lady janitor, to fifteen dollars a month;
to refuse the petition of the "Principle" to have his salary
raised from six hundred dollars to eight hundred dollars a
year. When the latter was reported to have used derogatory
words about the board members as a result of this niggard-
liness, he was made to appear before the board and retract
his words, and was "permitted" to finish out his term.

For more than twenty years James Roosevelt continued
his habit of tying his horse to the hitching-post outside the
red brick schoolhouse and stopping in to listen to the children's recitations. He took a paternal, almost feudal, interest in their education, and in their adjustment to the position in life to which they had been born. And, too, he liked
them because they were young and growing, for he had
always liked growing things. He was always kind and humorous with them, having that easy aproach to youth
that takes no account of years and offers only friendship.
Elderly men and women in Hyde Park still remember that
when the Sunday school class at St. James gathered to dec-

orate the church for Christmas, Mr. Roosevelt was often
with them and joined them in twining the greens.

The cleavage between his interest in public education in
the village and the education which he bestowed upon his
own son at once occurs to the modern reader. Why was
Franklin not sitting at one of the double desks in the red
brick schoolhouse in Hyde Park? The answer comes as
quickly as the thought. He did not attend the Hyde Park
school because it did not offer the kind of education that
his parents considered suitable for him, and because their
own schedule of travel made it impossible for him to go to
any school with regularity. Only once did he attend a formal elementary school, and that was in Bad Nauheim, Germany.

As the years went by, the Roosevelts always included this
quiet, rather stodgy Hessian spa in their itinerary. The
carbonated baths did Mr. Roosevelt a great deal of good, he
felt, and so from 1891 onward they visited Nauheim yearly,
usually staying at the Villa Britannia. Many of their English
and American friends also took the cure, and the society
was thoroughly congenial, especially after an English
church was established for the visitors.

The life here was pleasant but not exciting, regulated as
it was to elderly people who were not in the most vigorous
health. One drank the waters, one took the baths ordered by
one's physician, one went for walks of the exact length prescribed by him, one ate the diet that he recommended. In
the evening there was a concert—usually a good one—in
the Kurgarten, and at ten the patients were in bed.

It was not the most fascinating existence for a boy of nine,
and perhaps it was to provide an outlet for his overflowing
energy that the Roosevelts decided upon an experiment.

Franklin was sent, rather with tongue in cheek on the
part of his parents, to the Nauheim *Volksschule* (grade

school). He studied German reading, German dictation, the history of Siegfried, and arithmetic—briefly, without significant results.

Forty-two years later his *Volksschule* classmates sent to their old school friend, the President of the United States, a finely bound book, with pictures of his fellow pupils, of the teachers, of the school, and of the baths and fountains of Nauheim. These naïve and solid German businessmen and merchants were proud to claim acquaintance with Franklin Roosevelt in 1933.

The *Volksschule* did not set a precedent or open up a new school life for the boy. He remained under the care of his tutor, Mr. Arthur Dumper, until Groton could no longer be put off.

It cost Mrs. Roosevelt a heartsickening wrench to part with her fourteen-year-old son, even though he would be but a day's journey away. Life at Springwood was not full of comings and goings, of the jostling of many personalities, of coping with Papa's ferocious energy. That was Algonac; for Sara Delano Roosevelt life at Springwood was centered exclusively on two people—her husband and her son. The affection which in her youth had flowed out in so many directions had, since the birth of her one child, been drained into but two deep channels. It seemed as if she could hardly bear to break up the family circle.

Eighteen-ninety-six—that was the year the Parcae began to snip the threads in earnest. Mama Delano, worn out by that attack of typhoid from which she never fully recovered, closed her eyes forever, plunging "all hands," as she herself would have put it, into profound grief.

Two people whose lives would be bound inextricably with Springwood for the next fifty years, Mr. and Mrs. William Plog, coming to inquire about a situation for Mr. Plog as gardener, recall their first sight of Mrs. Roosevelt, walking down the stairs into the large central hall to meet them. She was dressed in deepest mourning for her mother, with a long black veil that hung below her shoulders. The Plogs (pronounced Plow) found the place to their liking and moved into the little gray house which stands today just behind the lot where visitors to the Home and Library park their cars. Mr. Plog took charge of the grounds—of the greenhouses and gardens, and of the thirty-inch Caldwell mower, horse-drawn, which was used to keep the lawns clipped short. Mrs. Plog, too young to be called "Mrs."—as Mrs. Roosevelt informed her—became "Josephine" and helped in the house. According to her, the house looked very much as it does now, if one forgets for the moment the additions that were made in 1915. The furniture in the music room was just the same, and the blue damask curtains hung at the windows, as they had done for nearly twenty years. The furniture in the South Parlor was upholstered in red, as it is today, and the old Dutch carved sideboard and clock, perpetual souvenirs of honeymoon days, stood where we see them now.

Although it is hard to judge the taste of a recently bygone day, Sara Roosevelt, even by the standards of 1880 and 1890, now so alien to us, could not have had that decorative finesse which pulls a room together and makes it seem harmonious. Her house was never lavishly furnished, in the sense that the Vanderbilts and Livingstons understood lavishness. It was not scantily furnished, for there was enough furniture, and what was there was solid. It was a house where color and form did not mean so much as sentiment and utility. The crowding pictures, vases, figurines, and bric-a-brac added nothing to the color harmonies and made the rooms seem full but awkwardly arranged.

Further, she was not the kind of housekeeper who tries out new groupings, moving furniture from spot to spot, to see if changing things around will work some magical improvement. New wallpapers, yes, and slipcovers when they were essential, but nothing that would materially alter the look of the house or strike her eye with unaccustomed novelty.

During her husband's lifetime there were but few exceptions to this inflexible rule. The front stairs were slightly remodeled; there was more veranda built on the southwest, and a deep bay window, facing west, was added to the dining room. A little room was built to open off that bay to the north. This was intended for a smoking room, but as the fireplace smoked more valiantly than could any coterie of gentlemen armed with Corona Coronas, this addition soon became a sort of glory hole, where piles of old magazines and books and guns and other odds and ends were dumped by Franklin and his father.

At the time of this remodeling an Italian mantel was set in the South Parlor, and a new wooden mantel was put in the upstairs morning room.

The people at Hyde Park grew used to seeing Mrs. Roosevelt in black. In 1898 Warren Delano, that indomitable man of action and kindly family monarch, at last succumbed to pneumonia. A broken hip had confined his body to a wheel chair since before the death of his wife; but no physical impediment could quench his energy and curiosity, and in 1893 he had taken a large party to Chicago to the World's Fair, wheel chair and all. He was nearly ninety when he died. Only James Roosevelt could approach in perfection Sallie's dear Papa, the model whom she had sought in every man.

The spring of 1900 saw Franklin graduated from Groton, preparing to enter Harvard in the fall. His father was really in delicate health this summer, with that frail, waxed look which come to the ailing aged. The strenuous sailing parties, the hunting and fishing, were over. Instead there was the sun on the veranda at Campobello, and quiet rides on Bobby, his favorite mount at Hyde Park.

The village children still stood when Mr. James Roosevelt, booted, riding crop in hand, mounted the platform beside the school principal's desk to hear them read and spell, and to watch them do their arithmetic on the blackboard. He spoke as precisely as ever—almost like an Englishman, they thought.

He still greeted the men on the place with old-fashioned courtesy. "Good morning, Clay." "Good morning, Plog. Have the seeds come from Thorburns?"

As late as November 9, Mr. Roosevelt took the chair at the monthly meeting of the Board of Education of Union Free School District No 1, Hyde Park. But in church, two Sundays before, the congregation had remarked how frail he looked as he handed the collection plate. Mrs. Roosevelt rented a cottage at Aiken, South Carolina, for the winter, in desperate anxiety to get him to a warmer climate, but it soon became apparent that he was too ill to take such a long journey. At the beginning of December it was decided to move the invalid to the Roosevelt apartment at the Hotel Renaissance, in order to have the best medical care.

At last even Mrs. Roosevelt was forced to recognize the fact that her husband was sinking rapidly. Although they lifted him into the carriage and took him for short drives, it was with his last strength that he looked upon the cool December streets of New York City.

Franklin was there, Rosy came, Aunt Laura Delano arrived to help. On December 8 James Roosevelt died, leaving his wife to wonder how she had lived through the moment of his going, and how she would endure life without him.

The obituary notices used the familiar phrase: "a gentleman of the old school."

V

Sara Roosevelt's Years Alone

THE wind blew cold the day James Roosevelt was buried at Hyde Park. It whipped out of the west, chilling
the schoolchildren who had come to pay a last tribute to
their friend. Although the sun shone, the pallbearers felt the
sharp gusts as they bore the coffin slowly out of the church
to the frozen graveyard. These were the men who worked
at Springwood, "the men on my place," as James Roosevelt
had requested in his will. His funeral was simple—the burial
service, the singing of three favorite hymns. And when the
guests from New York had gone, his wife and son turned
quietly back to the house at Hyde Park.

This was a day of desolation for Sara Roosevelt. Her affection, her hopes, her very reason for being had centered in
the husband who had so quietly slept away. She had with
fierce intensity drawn her whole world to a smaller and
smaller scale until, at the core of her life, there were just two
people—James Roosevelt and her son. With the death of his
father, eighteen-year-old Franklin was left entrenched alone
in the locked citadel of her heart. It was unnecessary for her
husband to have written into his will that his wife was to be
sole guardian of his son Franklin and that he wished the
boy to be under the influence of his mother. Sara Roosevelt
had for years been binding the boy to her with intelligent,

anxious, and dominant concern for every thought and action of his life.

Now alone at Hyde Park, she not only would have so to reshape her own existence that she could carry on the business of the Hyde Park estate as James had wished it done; she must also be a mother and father to their son, must help him make decisions, must alone guide him and advise him on how to play that role in life for which his heritage had qualified him.

Her sister Annie stayed with her at the first, and Franklin, of course, until it was time for him to return to Harvard. Kassie—now married, after the death of her first husband, Charles Robbins, to Hiram Price Collier—came up for a few days at a time to be with her. And finally Dora, leaving her second husband, Paul Forbes, in Europe, arrived to help Sara Roosevelt watch the winter go and wait for spring to brush softly over the valley of the Hudson.

The days were very much alike. The Delano sisters read aloud to each other—first *Paradise Lost,* then Longfellow's translation of Dante's *Divine Comedy.* Mrs. Roosevelt had all Franklin's stuffed birds out to dust and air, not trusting any of the maids with this precious collection. (It may be seen today behind the glass doors of the cabinet to the left of the entrance hall in the house at Hyde Park.) She had to lay in twenty tons more of coal to finish out the heating season. While the snow still lay on the roads, she arranged sleighrides for the servants.

The Delaware and Hudson Railroad sent a magnificent silver loving cup and tray to Mrs. Roosevelt, suitably inscribed as a "commemoration of Mr. Roosevelt's long connection with and services to the Company." Franklin wrote that he was much touched and that it was a thing they must always cherish.

Slowly, as the days grew warmer, the mistress of Springwood slipped into her husband's ways of doing things about the farm and keeping an eye everywhere out-of-doors. She rode Bobby, his favorite horse, around the place, watching the spring plowing. She and Dora helped Mr. Plog burn caterpillar nests all one May morning; she remarked that it ought to have been done in April. She was beginning to live again, to live in a pattern set by James Roosevelt, which, in the very act of consecrating it to him, she made indelibly her own.

When the summer came she and Franklin went abroad. They neither of them could bear the thought of Campobello. They did not want to go visiting. They did not want to spend the month of August at Hyde Park, when it usually becomes hot and steamy up and down the river. They joined forces with their old friends, Mrs. Alfred Pell, her daughter Frances, and Teddy Robinson, Theodore Roosevelt's nephew, on a cruise through the Norwegian fiords. Mrs. Roosevelt then toured through Germany and showed her son Dresden, where she had been to school, and other spots that she and his father had visited on their honeymoon—a sad-sweet reminiscence tour. Then they went through Switzerland and climbed up to Grand St. Bernard, where they spent the night in the desolate, cold, bare rooms of the monastery, dining on *"soupe au riz, nouilles,* etc."

The recipe for stewed dried fruit from the German lady must be from this journey, and possibly the *nouilles* or macaroni dish is the one served to them by the good monks. The rice soup preceding this on the menu was what the French called a *soupe maigre*—that is, a soup made without meat, a variety of cookery known at Algonac, where potato soup, onion soup, and rice soup had all been on the bill of fare.

The *nouilles* was probably the last entry in the Household Book for a year. There was, of course, no entertaining

at Hyde Park, beyond luncheon or dinner for a few intimate friends or members of the family, during the period
of mourning. In the winter of 1902, and again in the winter
of 1903, Mrs. Roosevelt moved to Boston for a few months,
in order to be near her son, for without him life was intol-
erably empty. At least in Boston her rooms were filled with
young people, and she could have Franklin's friends in for
tea, dinner, and supper.

Springwood, in all honesty, was not a gay house, nor had
it ever been during the days of Franklin's childhood. It had
been a happy house and a peaceful house, and the guests entertained there had known sincere hospitality. But the walls
had never bulged with dancing couples, nor the kitchen
passages echoed with the shouts of carefree young people
tearing along to the cold pantry to see what sort of snack
they could concoct at bedtime. In James' last year it had become an elderly and anxious house, with nurses tiptoeing
along the upper halls, and meals sent up on trays.

No wonder Sara Roosevelt found it hard to live here alone
during the harsh winter weather. In the spring she could be
outdoors, weeding the garden, picking pansies, taking her
early morning rides, walking in the woods, playing croquet;
and then the time was not so long until Franklin could come
home. She was curiously torn in those early days. She did
not want to travel alone at first; she was bitterly lonely at
Hyde Park by herself, and yet, now that it was hers, a very
tangible reminder of her husband, she began to refer to it as
"dear Hyde Park" and to take deeper root there than she
had ever done before.

She began also to be more active in village life. Before her
husband's death she had started a sewing class, having a
teacher come up from Wappingers Falls, a village south of
Poughkeepsie, to teach a selected group of eight pupils a
system of sewing. She herself counted as the eighth pupil

and, whenever she could, continued to go up on Saturdays to learn to backstitch and overcast, to French fell, gather, gusset, patch, tuck, and ruffle. She won first place with her "red hemming," a sort of overcast done with very small stitches on the right side of hemmed napkins and table linen with red thread, but seems not to have stood at the head of the class in the other more abstruse branches of the needlewoman's art.

This course was not merely an agreeable female pastime. Mrs. Roosevelt paid the teacher's salary and bought the materials used for the first year, in order to encourage the seven pupils to learn to teach also, so that a sort of voluntary, self-perpetuating sewing course might be held in the Hyde Park public school. The course lasted for twelve years, and one of the first gatherings invited to Springwood after Mr. Roosevelt's death was of the teachers and the sewing class, who came up one May afternoon for ice cream and cake. There are still in use some of the prizes Mrs. Roosevelt gave for attendance and good work—silver and gold scissors in velvet-lined red leather cases.

In the same spirit of community help, Mrs. Roosevelt started a cooking class, employing a teacher for a class of twelve girls. Mrs. Ashton, the wife of the rector of St. James church, kindly lent her kitchen for this further effort in vocational education, but the class seems not to have been very successful and was presently dropped.

She had for some time been on the board of trustees of a home for deaf mutes in Poughkeepsie, and now intensified her work there. In 1903 she drove down to the Home for a meeting, with her neighbors, the Newbolds, in their *automobile*. This was an innovation of which she did not entirely approve, although only two years later, when she moved to New York for the winter, she relaxed so far as to rent one of the then stylish and convenient "electrics," built

like a horse-drawn brougham and steered with a lever instead of a wheel.

This was a great concession to modernity for Sara Roosevelt. She had shown, in her social contacts, as well as in her
home, an increasing tendency to resist change of any kind.
It was not the result of the pathological clinging to the old
which many aging people display, but was a firm resistance
toward any innovation in usages and beliefs which she had
built up for herself and which she felt firmly and beyond
dispute were right. She did not, for example, accept an invitation to become a charter member of the Colony Club in
New York. She could not see any reason for a women's
club and would never have any reason to go inside one. She
never rode astride; it remained for Alice Roosevelt Long-
worth, on a visit to the Rogers estate, to be the first woman
in Hyde Park to be seen in trousers. And yet, how contradic-
tory! Sara Roosevelt loved to go coasting and spent two
hours, on New Year's morning in 1904, flying down the hills
at Springwood on a toboggan with Franklin, enjoying the
keen air on her face and the brisk, swift flight over the
smooth, packed snow. They frequently had the team hitched
up to pull them back to the top. A dignified widow of fifty,
and still getting her skirts bedraggled with snow as the sled
shot around curves, clinging to her son and laughing! It was
clearly the Delano energy, with some faint trace of that
eleven-year-old child who told her Auntie that she still enjoyed coasting after seven weeks of it, and had not yet had
enough.

The hours that mother and son spent together on this particular New Year's Day were poignant for both of them.
Franklin had recently dealt his mother a blow which nearly
shattered her emotionally, for all her strength and vigor. He
had told her at Thanksgiving time that he had asked his dis-
tant cousin, Anna Eleanor Roosevelt, to marry him, and

that now he was "the happiest man in the world." The thought of sharing Franklin was almost more than she could bear; her readjustment to a world without her husband had gone on very slowly; now to be asked to share her only remaining love—it was a jarring blow, a blow perhaps to her vanity, certainly to her devotion, that he should have thought of marrying anyone so soon.

In an old-fashioned, dramatic, and rather desperate gesture, she took her son and his friend Lathrop Brown on a cruise to the West Indies, leaving her "dear Hyde Park" in February. Franklin was to "think the engagement over." Franklin was tired and blue and in no mood to knuckle under to his mother's will. The engagement was announced early the following winter.

The plan for Franklin to study law at Columbia University after his graduation from Harvard would not be changed. But instead of having him to herself for long vacations at Hyde Park, or living with her in New York in the house she had taken at 200 Madison Avenue, his mother knew that she must watch while he set up a home of his own with someone else.

On St. Patrick's Day, five years after her "dear one left her," she attended her son's wedding. Theodore Roosevelt, the President of the United States, gave his orphaned niece away; Dr. Peabody of Groton read the marriage ceremony. All the Delanos were there, all the Theodore Roosevelt connections. Franklin was calm and happy; Eleanor was the same. Sara Roosevelt, erect and handsome in the beautiful black lace that had been her mother's, recognized this event for what it was, the first significant opposition to her way of life.

After the wedding the young couple left for Hyde Park to spend a week's honeymoon at Springwood before Franklin should have to go back to his law studies. Elespie welcomed them, as she had welcomed James Roosevelt and his bride. And Sara Roosevelt—characteristic touch—waited in her city house until she could go to their apartment and bring them home to lunch with her when the short week was over.

In June, as soon as Franklin had completed his law term, he and Eleanor went abroad for a two-month honeymoon; and while their letters flowed across the ocean to her, Mrs. Roosevelt was again left at Hyde Park to busy herself with the affairs of the house and of the farm. Now more than ever this was her own home—hers alone—so she laid her strong hand upon the reins; no smallest detail escaped her attention.

She bought a new bull, named Main Street of Anandale; she had a new well drilled (getting seven or eight gallons a minute at a hundred and twenty-three feet); she computed the produce from last season's harvest—235 bushels of rye, 582 bushels of oats, 7 bushels of wheat. She worked in the rose garden, got up early to ride and to arrange the flowers; she went out into the kitchen, lifted pot-lids, stirred puddings. Housekeeping details must now be sharply supervised.

Her excellent cook, Letitia Hayward, whose recipe for curry she treasured, had left to go home to England after having been at Springwood for eighteen months, and Hedda Johnson had taken her place. There was also a butler, who was changed fairly frequently since the faithful one-eyed Anderson had gone to Steen Valetje; a second man, a parlormaid, a kitchenmaid, and a laundress; with Elespie, of course, and a personal maid. Calder, the personal maid she had had for many years, never got on well with Elespie, and there was household friction, which Mrs. Roosevelt, who always acted as her own executive housekeeper at Hyde Park, was at some pains to obliterate. In the end it was always Elespie who won out. She had now become so deaf that she had resorted to a marvelous homemade ear trumpet contrived out of an old dipper and kept upon a shelf in the kitchen. She swore she could hear perfectly if one shouted into the dipper, but guests could hardly be expected to roar, "Get your dipper, Elespie!" and so she was transferred from chambermaid to parlormaid, to kitchenmaid, to the laundry. In 1908 this faithful servant went back to her family in Canada, honorably retired, the only one of all the people on the place mentioned by James Roosevelt in his will, the only living bridge back to the days when Springwood was young.

The household routine begun in the early days was now carried out with precision. Each servant received a small paper-bound notebook, in which his or her duties were written down. He (or she) also received a wage-book, in which cash payments were entered as they were made, usually once a month, the entry constituting a receipt. After breakfast had been served to Mrs. Roosevelt in her morning room, the cook came up to discuss the menus for the day and receive her orders. In the early days Mrs. Roosevelt herself had handed out the household stores and the linen for daily use, but latterly this practice was stopped. She frequently did the shopping herself, however, patronizing a grocer in Poughkeepsie and a Hyde Park butcher. The produce from the farm continued to supply the table at Springwood, as well as in New York, with butter, fruit, vegetables, milk, and cream.

The duties of the footman or second man, as outlined by Mrs. Roosevelt, furnish an excellent basis on which to reconstruct the operation and management of the house at Hyde Park. Every day his early duties were to open doors and shutters and windows, carry up coal and wood to the kitchen and laundry, clean and fill the kerosene lamps, and clean shoes—as in European households, members of the family and guests left their shoes outside their bedroom doors to be shined by a member of the household staff. He was then to sweep and wash the porches, and clean the service hall and the back stairs and back porch. He was to help in the pantry with the breakfast dishes and, when the parlormaid was in the dining room waiting on table, to help in the pantry. Weekly he was to clean and polish the doorknobs and brasses. He was to clean a few windows each week and wipe and brush the screens. It was also his specific duty to freeze the ice-cream (one can only hope that occasionally he had an opportunity to lick the dasher).

Complementing the footman's duties on the first floor, the parlormaid was assigned the care of the rooms there, except the dining room and smoking room. As suggested in the Household Book, she was to wipe the hardwood floors daily "with a broom with a canton flannel cover tied over it." She was to answer the doorbell and telephone daily, while the butler was dressing, and on his afternoon off. When the family was at home, or there were visitors, she was to help the butler serve lunch and dinner, also to help with the dishes. And after the grandchildren began to fill the house with clamor and childish shouting, it was the parlormaid's duty to serve the children's supper in the nursery.

The rooms on the upper floor were under the care of a chambermaid. The laundress, who reigned in the laundry house, a small wooden box of a place close to the kitchen door—with a girl to help her turn the mangle and man the washboards—saw to it that the linen closets were kept filled with freshly washed and ironed sheets and pillowcases—percale for the guest rooms, initialed linen sheets and square linen pillowcases for Mrs. Roosevelt's room. This fresh, clean linen, smelling of good Dutchess County air and sunshine, was packed in baskets and brought to the second floor, where the chambermaid put it away—the bedlinen, the linen handtowels initialed SDR, the white bathtowels with the large red R on them. Mrs. Roosevelt's personal linen, washed and ironed by the laundress, was, of course, mended and put away by her personal maid.

The last laundress at Springwood to keep the Roosevelt household clean and ironed is today a member of the housekeeping staff at Hyde Park, under the auspices of the National Park Service. She remembers the very fine handkerchief-linen and silk lingerie she used to "do up" for Mrs. Roosevelt, and how Madam (Mrs. Roosevelt was always called Madam by her staff) used to come out to the laundry for a little visit and watch her as she heated the irons on a wide ledge built around the old-fashioned coal stove. Electricity was not installed at Springwood until 1908, so that what we today think of as essential modern housekeeping appliances were not in use until some time after that date. Mrs. DePew, the laundress, did not get an electric washing machine or mangle until after 1918.

With a smoothly functioning household such as this, it was possible to move the staff back and forth between Hyde Park and 200 Madison Avenue, or Hyde Park and Campobello, with ease and efficiency, and to entertain over the weekend, or at formal dinners, with a certain American-European elegant plainness.

Mrs. Roosevelt's dinners were usually served to eight or ten guests, more often than not members of the family or very old friends. Her favorite table decorations were Hyde Park roses and carnations, or roses and freesias—sent down from the Springwood greenhouse, if she were entertaining in New York—arranged in a large centerpiece, with individual blooms at each place. She sat at the head of the rectangular table, and her son at the foot, whenever he could be present. Both butler and parlormaid served.

A typical menu would include grapefruit, clear soup, halibut with hollandaise sauce, chicken timbales with asparagus, filet of beef with string beans and potatoes, squab in

aspic, artichoke salad, and ice cream. For the entertainment
of Governor John Alden Dix of New York, for example, or
to celebrate other special occasions, the guest list might be
increased to sixteen, but the menu (written in French in
Mrs. Roosevelt's delicate slanting handwriting) would be
but a slight variation from the above. Silver, damask—the
long white linen cloths and square napkins then in vogue—
crystal, cut glass, and dishes were carried back and forth between Hyde Park and the town house, with the exception,
of course, of such everyday items as were in constant use in
both places.

The Franklin Roosevelts lived very close to 200 Madison
Avenue—right around the corner on East-Thirty-sixth Street
—and there was constant coming and going between the
two houses, particularly that first year of their marriage. In
May 1906 Franklin's first child was born, a little girl named
Anna for her maternal grandmother, and eighteen months
later Sara Roosevelt had the joy of knowing that the dear
name James would be handed on to a grandson. She was delighted with her grandchildren, and showered upon them
the attention and affection which grandmothers almost always provide. The babies were often with her—all five of
them, as they came along—and she found them "sweet and
dear." The beginning of this important change in family
history is recorded in the Household Book with the entry of
a recipe for oatmeal for Anna, and with a list of breakfast
cereals for Anna and James. The knitting directions for a
child's jersey and for a baby jacket were doubtless used for
the grandchildren. Nannie Church's baby socks with col-
ored stripes, which were quite the thing in the eighties,
would hardly have been right in 1906 and 1907.

In the summertime the Franklin Roosevelts took the babies
to Campobello. Mrs. Franklin was a competent mother and
had an excellent nurse. It was not that Sara Roosevelt was

not wanted; but she could see that she was not needed. Since there was no one now except herself whose comfort and convenience had to be consulted, she turned to a habit of many years' standing. In 1907 she sailed to England again, a trip which picked up the threads of her many European friendships and re-established the pleasant custom of spending a few months every now and then with her sister Dora and the Forbes family in Paris, or with English friends.

It was at this time that Mrs. O'Callaghan contributed her superb recipe for mincemeat to the Household Book.

Although Mrs. Philip Martineau's recipe for Devonshire cream does not occur until some pages later, Mrs. Roosevelt wrote Franklin and Eleanor that she had met the Martineaus on this same visit. Philip Martineau was a cousin of Cyril Martineau, the husband of Kassie's daughter, Muriel Robbins.

"Fay's" recipe for *fromage à la crème* would also fit into this 1907 trip, for Mrs. Roosevelt spent much time with her sister Dora, and Fay was Fay Forbes, Dora's sister-in-law. Miss Forbes lived in Paris because she had once braved an ocean voyage to get there, so the family story ran, and felt she could never live through another one to get home, a pleasant form of locomania if one prefers to live in Paris— and that was the Golden Age in Paris, as elsewhere on the Continent and in America.

Upon her return from abroad Mrs. Roosevelt became engrossed with the finishing of a new town house—or, more correctly, two new town houses, one for herself and one for Franklin. She had purchased the property on East Sixty-fifth Street and was building adjoining homes at numbers 47 and 49. They were four stories high, of stone and brick, with iron balconies off the second stories. An arrangement of double doors between the drawing rooms at the backs of the second floors permitted the two houses to be thrown together for entertaining. The dining rooms on the floor below also opened into each other. The same front vestibule served both houses.

Franklin and his increasing family lived here for two years. In 1910 he was elected State Senator from Dutchess County, and they moved to Albany. In 1913, just before he was to begin his second term in the legislature, Josephus Daniels asked him to become Assistant Secretary of the Navy, and the Roosevelts moved to Washington. There was always Campobello for the children's summer months; and there was the house at Hyde Park. In his early political campaigns Franklin made it his headquarters. This was the first faint eddy of the political whirlpool which would engulf the old house on the Hudson, and which introduced into Sara Roosevelt's home a swelling army of strangers, who came not because she had invited them, nor, indeed, because she wished to offer them hospitality, but to carry on the articulate business of politics with her son.

It was not what Sara Roosevelt had planned for herself or for Franklin. The house at Hyde Park was to have been the center from which their joint activities could spread in comfortable directions, and not a spot to which he returned only for rest, spiritual refreshment, and political necessity. And yet, could it have been otherwise? All observations and observers seem to agree that his mother's responsibilities and management of Springwood could have brooked no second in command; refusing to yield to her son, she kept a firm and undisputed hold upon the activities of the farm, insisting that it be run in every detail as had been done in her husband's time.

Her brother Warren's advice and help she occasionally took. He supplied her with the formula for good cheap roofing paint which appears in the Household Book, and he would come down from Barrytown to start her alfalfa—

eighty quarts of seed to an acre and a half. But the formula
to help laying hens, the feed for chickens in the winter, the
notes about sowing red clover to improve the land, and the
fertilizer mixture for cherry and peach trees, these bear wit-
ness that the farm was as much her concern as the house itself. As a gentleman's occupation, overseeing farm operations had been a useful and pleasant diversion in her husband's and his grandfather's time. It furnished Sara Roosevelt
with an outlet for some of her extaordinary Delano energy,
and was a noticeable signpost to the increasing "setness" of
her ways. As wages increased and prices of feed, fertilizer,
and seed went up, her farm income ran steadily behind expenses, but she refused to give up farming operations. Her
husband had always managed a farm!

The cooking recipes, the household hints, the farm notes,
and the knitting directions, which follow each other in no
particular order from 1907 onward, tell the story. Even Mrs.
Roosevelt's firm will could not keep her own world an-
chored to the nineties. Franklin's children were gradually
growing up and changing the atmosphere in her own home.
Her grandchildren came to Hyde Park, as the small Delanos
had gone to Fairhaven; but the subdued and decorous be-
havior of her own childhood generation, and even the man-
nerly and obedient little Franklin, had not prepared her for
the lively boys and girls who tramped mud into her kitchen,
raced up and down stairs, dug furiously in their own small
vegetable gardens until they got bored with it, helped with
the haying if they felt like it, and went about dressed in dirty
blue jeans.

In 1915, before the United States entered World War I,
Mrs. Roosevelt agreed with Franklin that the house needed
to be bigger—much bigger. The architectural firm of Hop-
pin and Koen were engaged to make plans for a major remodeling, in order to make the house more commodious

and suitable for her son. The result was an adroit combination of old and new, Victorian and modern, which met the family's needs, and which left Mrs. Roosevelt still the mistress of a house not too unpleasantly different from the home to which she had come as a bride.

The old tower which had been Franklin's upstairs schoolroom was changed to give a full third floor, with bedrooms, bathrooms, and nursery. On the second floor, above a big new library, was Mrs. Roosevelt's bedroom and bath. She wanted the same outlook to the southeast that she had enjoyed in her old room, so that she could see who was coming from the Post Road to the front door. Her son and his wife occupied two bedrooms, dressing room, and bath in the same wing. From his bed Franklin Roosevelt could look down the Hudson over a view not quite so full of poetic grandeur as that which had intrigued Andrew Jackson Downing at Algonac, but a vista which showed "the River" winding placidly toward Poughkeepsie.

The rooms along the west side of the main hall remained much as they had been—the "pink room," with the trellised wallpaper which Mrs. Roosevelt had selected while Franklin was in college, and which still gives a faded air of prettiness to this old-fashioned chamber; the "chintz room," and the little guest room over the smoking room, cold in winter and hot in summer, as it had always been. The curtains were of white embroidered Swiss organdy, as always.

On the other side of the hall, Franklin's boyhood room was not changed; but Mrs. Roosevelt's morning room became a guest room, as did the one in which her son was born. It was necessary to sacrifice the west ends of these rooms to make a corridor through to the new addition, so that old Dr. Parker would hardly have recognized the bedroom in which he had assisted Sara Roosevelt's son into the world. Seven baths were added during the alterations—a much-needed improvement, since the family bathroom and one bath in the servants' quarters were decidedly no longer adequate.

Downstairs, the old cold pantry gave way to a more modern ice-chest, the space it had occupied being added to the butler's pantry and a door cut into the north end of the dining room, so that it was no longer necessary to carry dishes from the kitchen out into the hall and then through the east dining-room door. The servants' sitting room was added to the kitchen space, and the new fireproof addition on the north contained a larger room for the staff, as well as the children's schoolroom—later President Roosevelt's study. Cooking arrangements were substantially the same, with a wood-and-coal range and, at a much later date, an artificial-gas stove.

The front hall, the dining room, the music room—these remained much as they had been in the older house. Only the South Parlor was radically altered. This was cut in half to make a passageway from the main hall to the large stone addition on the south. The east half became Mrs. Roosevelt's morning room or Snuggery. Of the whole house this dark little parlor, still furnished with red-upholstered chairs and crowded with pictures and bric-a-brac, was most peculiarly her own. Here she liked to have her breakfast served. She had her desk in this room, where she kept her accounts and paid her bills. The household staff came here for their orders, and here she poured tea for people who happened to drop in near four o'clock.

Even so comprehensive a remodeling did not alter the appearance of the furnishings to any great degree, although the beautiful old mahogany sofa and side chairs which had graced the South Parlor since Rebecca Roosevelt's day were, alas, re-upholstered by Mrs. McGowan, the caretaker who came down from Campobello to look after the house when the family was away in the wintertime. She covered the horsehair with chintz, and the set was then moved up to the children's domain on the third floor.

The house was not redecorated in the modern sense, or, with one important exception, provided with additional furniture. The rich blue damask curtains still hung at the windows of the music room, as they had since Sara Roosevelt first put them up soon after her marriage. The flowered chintz now in this room was not purchased by Sara Roosevelt until 1939, shortly before the visit of the King and Queen of England.

The Paul Troubetzkoy statue of Franklin, made in 1911 at the order of his godmother, Nelly Blodgett, again stood in the front hall. The portrait of Sara Roosevelt, painted by the sculptor's brother, Pierre, in 1900, was hung beside a portrait of her husband by Moscheles, in the passageway leading from the front hall to the new library. The two Troubetskoys were friends of Mrs. Roosevelt, and since the sculptor, Paul, was famous for his cooking, and particularly for his risotto, one is tempted arbitrarily to assign the recipe for this dish to him. The brothers were Russian and styled themselves princes. An Italian recipe prepared by a Russian prince has a fetching cosmopolitan connotation which is difficult to resist.

It was only as one walked past these portraits and the door of the Snuggery that the house suddenly lost its old flavor. The taste of a new generation at once became apparent in the new south wing.

The historian at the Franklin D. Roosevelt National Historic Site, Mr. George Y. Wilkins of the National Park Service, believes that the inspiration for this room came directly from Sir Hugh and Lady Cholmeley's home at Grantham, England. Franklin certainly wrote to his mother, when he visited there in 1903, that the house was "a dream of

Nirvana, & as the situation much resembles ours, I am taking notes & measurements of everything.—What a house! The family must have thought me crazy to rubber so at the pictures & Library for it was *almost* my model library—with three distinct parts and yet all thoroughly liveable and satisfactory."

The large oak-paneled addition to Springwood does indeed answer this description. A Gilbert Stuart portrait of Isaac the Patriot looks down from above one fireplace; and an Inman portrait of his son James adorns the mantel at the opposite end of the room—both framed in wood carvings, after the style of Grinling Gibbons. The upholstered furniture is so arranged that there is a conversation grouping at each end and one in the middle. And though the walls are lined with books, the atmosphere is that of an informal living room, not that of a quiet and secluded spot for study. The old bracketed porches to the south and east gave way before these innovations, and were replaced by a large screened porch at the south end of the living-library. A pillared portico was added to the front, and a coat of yellow stucco—a color of which Mr. Andrew Jackson Downing would have approved—covered the clapboards of the old Wheeler home.

The house at Hyde Park belonged legally to Sara Roosevelt. It had belonged to her in many other ways as well—emotionally and temperamentally, if a house may be said to have a temperament. After 1915 her name still stood upon the deed, but the atmosphere and feeling of the place changed with its outward appearance.

The war for which she knitted helmets and noted a recipe for durable Canadian war cake helped to widen the increasing gap between James Roosevelt's widow and contemporary American thinking. But it was her own rigid adherence to the standards of the past—in the furnishings of both her house and her mind—which forced a broader and broader cleavage between her son's generation and herself. She would not let go of the old; she refused to grasp at the new. She was not being quaintly old-fashioned as her husband and his father and his grandfather had been. She was determined to demonstrate as forcibly as she knew how that her ideas and standards were right, and that those who disagreed with her were wrong.

A second painfully bitter opposition to her judgment failed to shake her. In 1921 her beloved son Franklin came down with infantile paralysis, which deprived him of the use of his legs and confined him to sedentary occupations for the rest of his life. Sara Roosevelt wanted to bring him back permanently to Hyde Park—to reinstate him in the life of a country gentleman and amateur scholar such as his grandfather, Dr. Isaac, had enjoyed. Her country home was the place for him in this frightful affliction, she felt; that was the only kind of existence she could conceive of for the invalid he had become.

Franklin's wife and his old friend, the imaginative and sagacious Louis McHenry Howe, as well as that able physician and schoolmate, Dr. George Draper, opposed this capitulation to the enemy with all the strength that they could muster. Aided by FDR's own magnificent will, they defeated Sara Roosevelt. Only the remarkable myopia of the strong-willed prevented her from perceiving that it would have been impossible for her son, at the age of thirty-nine, with many years of active public life behind him, to revert wholly to the country-squire interests which his father and grandfather had found acceptable. It is true that a nostalgic allegiance to this environment remained with him all his life. That he did not yield to it and to his mother's well-intentioned persuasion made history.

Within two years Mr. Roosevelt was back, as vice-president

in charge of the New York office of the Fidelity and De-
posit Company of Maryland. He had resigned from his post
in the Navy to run for Vice-President on the Democratic
ticket with Cox, and was beaten. Consequently, it was to
private business, and law practice with Basil O'Connor as
well, that this energetic and gregarious man returned, whom
his mother's exaggerated maternal solicitude and almost
physical devotion would have condemned to be a useless invalid.

There are many people still living in Hyde Park, besides
those employed at the Franklin D. Roosevelt National Site,
who vividly remember Mrs. Roosevelt. Even though she
had many friends and was almost constantly with some
member of her family, oddly enough the impression one
gets from those who knew her, or worked for her, is that
she was a lonely woman after 1921. Her son was frequently
away on business, swimming for his health at Warm Springs,
Georgia, or boating in Florida for the same reason. Her
daughter-in-law had become much interested in politics.
Her grandchildren were growing fast and occupied with
their own interests.

Many a long evening she had a pile of opera records
brought into the front hall, and there, sitting by the Edison
Victrola, which was most uncomfortably placed behind
the cabinet to the left of the front door, she would have the
butler wind the machine for her while she played all the
great arias. When the radio had been perfected to the ear-
phone stage, she would sit alone in the Snuggery, listening
to the wonders of the wireless.

People saw her in the village and would return her greet-
ings pleasantly, but these were different days from those
when James Roosevelt had ridden up the village street, lift-
ing his hat and bowing, and every child had bowed back. A
local story goes that Mrs. Roosevelt once offered to give a

ride to some village boys while she was out driving along
the Post Road.

"No," they said.

"Do you want a ride?" she repeated.

"No," they said, puzzled and probably a bit self-conscious.

"No, thank you!" she said with emphasis, and drove on.

There is a story, too, that during a Republican administration the postmaster—by the authority of the postal rules and
regulations, one presumes—decided to close the Hyde Park
post office on Sunday. Mrs. Roosevelt objected strenuously to
this new practice, and did her best to have it opened again.
But the six-day week for the postmaster won out—he had a
point of view which perhaps had not occurred to her.

Locally her many kindnesses are gratefully remembered.
She gave money to needy families (usually through the minister of St. James Church); she took care of families where
sickness had struck hard; she helped young people with
their education; she remembered to bring little things back
from Europe with her, as gifts for "the people on my place."
Turkeys were sent out at Christmas, as well as other presents (always white-tissue-wrapped). This was the rule for
many years, as one beneficiary remembers, and with this
holiday largesse went some of the most wonderful striped
stick candy a child ever drooled over.

Because people like the Roosevelts had so much and, by
comparison, those living around them had so little, such
philanthropy from the top down was not always a good
thing. Mrs. Roosevelt herself recognized this, and said that
"we," meaning herself and her friend Mrs. Archie Rogers,
"are making beggars of the people up in the village."

Since this was her viewpoint, and because she was
strongly against anything so commercial as incorporation,
Mrs. Roosevelt's project of building a library in Hyde Park
to the memory of her husband was not a long-term success.

A remarkable situation arose which has probably seldom
been duplicated in other small communities when people of
means decided to put up a library memorial—a form of
philanthropy which had become an accepted and popular
American tradition.

In 1926 Mrs. Roosevelt purchased land on the Post Road
a short distance from where the old red brick schoolhouse
stood, and then put up a gray fieldstone library, with the
name of her husband carved in stone over the doorway. This
was for the use of the schoolchildren and residents of
Hyde Park, and was such a memorial as James Roosevelt
himself might have liked. The homelike room, with its
many shelves and open fireplace, is today most pleasing and
invites the casual reader to stay and browse. But Hyde Park
was and is not a wealthy community, with the exception of
the "river families." It was never able to raise enough money
to pay all the running expenses of this worthy but rather
arbitrary gift. During her lifetime Sara Roosevelt continued
to pay all expenses in excess of the $3500 collected in mem-
bership dues. After her death in 1941, her son maintained it,
and after his death his family sold it to the town of Hyde
Park for $4500.

It became the Hyde Park Free Library, and now places a
heavier financial burden on the community than is comfortable. Franklin Roosevelt always felt that the only practical way to run the library was to have the money taken
from either town taxes or the school district taxes—but the
citizens of the townships concerned did not wish to do this.
And so this memorial to a kindly man who was greatly interested in children and their education has ceased to have
its original meaning, and stands a small monument to the
changes in men's social outlook.

It was not the only memorial to James Roosevelt. Scottish
granite was brought across the Atlantic for the solid polished

grave-sized block which rests over his burying place; and a window in St. James Church gives "thanks to God for the beloved memory of James Roosevelt."

Memorials and stones and windows were one expression of Sara Roosevelt's deep love for the husband who had been dead so many years. Her devout adherence to his principles of honesty and simplicity was another. In many ways she also saw Franklin as a living memorial to the father from whom he had inherited humor, warmth, and an inquiring mind.

The son's affection for his mother was always profound. In later years, as he grew away from her in some respects, he became closer to her in others; and the fact that he recognized her intent to dominate did not dry up the springs of filial love. Neither did it prevent his making decisions for himself. He accepted the nomination for Governor of New York on the Democratic ticket, and he put on a campaign which proved to himself, to his mother, and to the country that he had won his fight with infantile paralysis. Mrs. Roosevelt now began to make the remark that has been so often quoted: "I don't want my boy to run for office— but if he does, I hope he wins."

After he became Governor, although she never ceased to try to influence him, he moved into arenas of action where his mother could not follow. With the great pressure of affairs upon him, he could not adapt himself to her as he had done, though the bond between them was still close and strong. In her old age, inch by inch, his mother began to yield to the demands of her son's position in politics, and to the necessity for altering the scheme of life at Hyde Park.

It was not possible, now, to plan small intimate dinners and family luncheons, as she had done; strangers were constantly in need of food and overnight lodging, and when her son was at Hyde Park there were secretaries and telephone operators and a persistent stream of visitors. When one considers the degree to which her privacy was invaded, it is impossible not to express the highest admiration for this lady —and the word is used in its old-fashioned sense—who could yet adapt herself to contact with the men and women of all social classes who were gradually pre-empting the leisure as well as the spare bedrooms at Springwood.

The passing years extorted even crueler adjustments. In 1920 her brother Warren, always so helpful to her, had met with a shocking accident in a train and carriage collision, which cost him his life. Her sister Annie, after a long and useful life at Algonac, full of good works and kindliness, died suddenly in 1926. Algonac itself was not the old house. It was a replica built when a fire destroyed everything but the shell of the original building in 1916. An incredible amount of household furnishings, objets d'art, and personal possessions were saved because the fire started on the top floor and took five hours to burn downward; but still, the very home in which Sara Delano had been born, in which she had spent her childhood and so many years of her young ladyhood, in which she had continued hopefully the entries in her Household Book—this was gone.

And as to her home at Hyde Park, it too was an old frame about a new picture. The current parlormaid, in her fresh-starched cotton dress, still murmured, "Good morning, Madam," when her mistress came down to the Snuggery for breakfast. Mr. Plog still produced scented masses of bloom from the gardens and the greenhouse—rich pink Baroness Rothschild roses, crimson General Jacqueminots, bright Magna Chartas, and the pansies which Mrs. Roosevelt always wanted to see in the borders. The setting itself, and the faces of her "people on the place," these had not changed.

But broughams and victorias no longer rolled up the driveway from the Albany Post Road, and time had taken many of her old friends. There were fewer casual visitors for tea to taste the crumbly moonshines or the hearty six-egg tea cake. Instead, disturbing—if not unpleasant—as she must have found it, buses from Poughkeepsie drove up to Sara Roosevelt's door and disgorged visitors by the hundreds. There had been hordes of people swarming about the house in 1920, during Franklin's vice-presidential campaign. Now this public invasion began anew in 1929 with a visit from the Women's Trade Union League and officials of the State Federation of Labor. Governor and Mrs. Roosevelt, and the Governor's mother, Mrs. James Roosevelt, were hosts to this group and spectators of the pageant which was staged on the south lawn overlooking the Hudson. The pageant depicted the early struggles of the Women's Trade Union League, the strikes led by the organization, and its many conflicts with employers and the police. The trumpets before the walls of Jericho could blow no louder blast than this.

In the spring of 1931 Mrs. Roosevelt made reservations for her sister Dora Forbes and herself on the French Line steamship *Paris*. She was just going to "run over to Europe," as she phrased it, for one of her frequent early summer trips. No sooner had the ladies arrived in Paris than Mrs. Roosevelt developed pnuemonia, following an attack of influenza. She was so ill that Mrs. Forbes communicated with Governor Roosevelt, and the newspapers made much of his swift trip across the Atlantic to his mother's bedside. She had always been robust, and this was one of the first serious illnesses in her life; pneumonia at the age of seventy-seven gave genuine cause for worry. Fortunately there were no ill effects, and Mrs. Roosevelt returned on the *Paris* on June 9, with some very distinguished fellow-passengers, among them Martinelli, the Metropolitan tenor; Mayor James M.

Curley of Boston and his daughter; and Miss Texas Guinan
with thirty night-club girls, who had not been permitted to
land in France or England.

The recipe for crêpes "c'est Paris" is printed on a leaflet
which was inserted in the pages of the Household Book,
and there is nothing to say whether Mrs. Roosevelt tasted the
dessert on the voyage over or on her return journey. One
would like to think that Miss Guinan enjoyed this delicacy
too.

This is the last entry to which a positive date can be assigned. The small notebook was nearly full, and there was
no room to add items currently useful in the new life upon
which "plane Sarah Delano" was entering, close to the age
of eighty. "Lemonade and Cup Cakes for 900" or "Sand-
wiches and Tea for 500" would have looked strange written
on the pages of Sarah Alvey Delano's small gift. The mother
of the Governor of New York had little use for homely
recipes and remedies.

State troopers were at her gates, and hundreds of
unknown partisans streamed across her lawn, shouting and
carrying torches and banners.

The story of Sara Delano Roosevelt's Household Book
ends here—two years before the United States Secret Service
moved its operatives stealthily into the bushes and shrubbery
around the house at Hyde Park and posted a guard outside
the door of Franklin's room.

One cannot keep a household book for a house that belongs
to the nation.

Family Album

A SELECTION OF PICTURES TAKEN MAINLY FROM
THE DELANO AND ROOSEVELT FAMILY COLLECTIONS,
MANY OF THEM HERETOFORE UNPUBLISHED;
FOLLOWED BY TWO FACSIMILE PAGES FROM THE
HOUSEHOLD BOOK

Grateful acknowledgment is made to the Franklin D. Roosevelt Library for permission to reproduce all of the following except the engraving of Mount Hope.

SARA DELANO

at about the time of her marriage to James Roosevelt. This large studio photograph, in a heavy frame, now hangs in one of the third-floor bedrooms of the house at Hyde Park.

MR. and MRS. WARREN DELANO II
and
ALGONAC,
their "Hudson River bracketed" home on the west bank above Newburgh, where Sara was born

SARA with her brother Philippe, 1862

SARA in her teens

SARA on her white mare at Algonac, 1873

Laura   Sara   Kassie

Annie   Dora

THE FIVE DELANO SISTERS, 1883

JAMES ROOSEVELT in 1879

SARA   DELANO   ROOSEVELT

(taken in Rome during their honeymoon, 1881)

DR. ISAAC ROOSEVELT, grandfather of the President and father of James, from an oil painting in the dining room of the house at Hyde Park

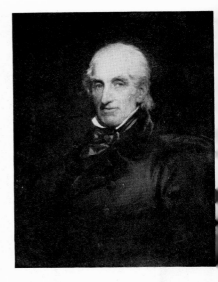

MOUNT HOPE, in Poughkeepsie, just below Hyde Park; from an engraving of the home of James Roosevelt, F.D.R.'s great-grandfather, where Dr. Isaac (above) was probably born, and where F.D.R.'s father lived before it was destroyed by fire in 1866

(Dutchess County Historical Society.)

JAMES ROOSEVELT at the kitchen entrance to Springwood; the stable in the background

THE HYDE PARK PUBLIC SCHOOL, to which James Roosevelt gave much attention

SPRINGWOOD, south view; James Roosevelt on the veranda

"THE HUDSON RIVER FROM THE RESIDENCE OF JAMES ROOSEVELT, ESQ. AT HYDE PARK, N. Y." looking south from the terrace shown above; this old print was a favorite of F.D.R.

SPRINGWOOD, east view, before the remodeling

SPRINGWOOD TODAY, same view as in the photograph above; the old house remains almost intact within the new.

SOUTH PARLOR, later Sara Roosevelt's "Snuggery"

MUSIC ROOM ("Dresden Room") looking through into the dining room

FRANKLIN with each of his parents, in Washington, 1887

FRANKLIN, about age 9, with James and Sara on the lawn at Springwood

MRS. CAREY

DR. EDWARD H. PARKER

NANCY F. CHURCH
("Cousin Nannie")

SARAH ALVEY DELANO ("Aunt Sarah")

SARA DELANO ROOSEVELT and JAMES ROOSEVELT, about 1900

Pan Dowdy —

Pare & quarter apples &
put them in a brown
earthenware crock —

Add 1 cup of molasses
1 tablespoonful of cinamon
a little sugar & water
enough to moisten —

Cover with cream of tartar
paste — Bake slowly
from 2 to 3 hours, then
break the paste in &
serve cold —

from Mrs James Lawrence
Groton

List for Layette from Marian Low.
1881.

12. night slips
12. simple dresses
4 day flannel petticoats
4 night   "   "
3 od dozen small diapers
3 or 4   "   large   "
12 white petticoats
12 pair of socks
fine flannel to tear into Bands
12 aprons to hold rubber cloth
3 flannel aprons for nurse
6 knit shirts

6 pillow cases
6 crib sheets
2 mattress covers.

their complete
it sent 40
dresses are
280 yards com-
menced flannel
yard wide 1 in
dispensation -

THE TEXT OF THE HOUSEHOLD BOOK

Sara Delano
from S. A. D.

Fair Haven
29. Aug. '79.

[*S. A. D.—Sarah Alvey Delano*]

[*A partial index which Sara Delano Roosevelt wrote into the front pages of the Household Book has been omitted here. Otherwise the contents have been reproduced word for word, with editors' notes added in brackets [ ]. Entries marked with an asterisk are treated more fully in the section called "Notes for Cooks" which follows. A complete listing of the entries by subject will be found in the Index at the end of the book.*]

H. W.'s receipt for Orange Marmalade

To every pound of oranges put 2 quarts of water, boil them 2 hours or until you can run a straw through, cut them into thin slices taking out only pips— For every pound of fruit put 2 pounds of sugar and half a pint of the water in which the oranges were boiled— While you are cutting the fruit, pour the water over the sugar, let it stand to dissolve— When the fruit is ready, put the sugar on and boil till quite clear— Add the fruit and boil half an hour.

Harriet Wood's receipt—Fairhaven, Sept. 1879

[*Harriet Wood—Sarah Alvey Delano's housekeeper and companion, later housekeeper at Algonac.*]

Poulet au macaroni

¾ lb. minced cold roast or stewed chicken
2½ oz. minced ham
  2 table spoon full of gravy
¼ tea spoon of grated nutmeg
¼ lb. fine bread crumbs
a small piece of butter, a little chopped mushroom, &
truffle or grated lemon peel, & two eggs to bind it.
2 ounzes of Macaroni.

Proceed thus:

First mix the chicken & ham & add the gravy, season with
pepper & salt, add the nutmeg & bread crumbs, then the
mushrooms or grated peel, then the two eggs & beat all well
together & make the forcemeat.

In the meantime, boil the macaroni in salt & water & drain
it.

Butter a mould & line it carefully with macaroni starting
in the middle (& garnishing if you wish to).

When the mould has been lined, fill it full of the force
meat & cover it with a plate or small dish, steam it for a half
an hour. Turn out carefully & serve with a good gravy *or*
white sauce poured around it—(*not over*).

This makes enough for ten or twelve people— A tin mould
like a charlotte tin will serve.

This dish is much prettier if the macaroni is cut in small
pieces & the bowl lined with it, it takes more time but looks
like honeycomb.

A. L. D. H.'s receipt tried by her in Shanghi, Jan. 15th, /79.

Aspic Jelly

Put in a stew pan two calves feet chopped in pieces, a ham bone *or* some slices of ham or bacon, any remains of game (*not* high) or poultry you may have *or* uncooked meat, 1 or 2 onions, 1 or 2 carrots cut in slices, 1 clove, sweet herbs, whole pepper & salt—

Add a cup of cold water or broth, cover the stewpan & put it on a brisk fire, shaking it occasionally. When the meat begins to take color put in another cup of hot water or broth & in a half-hour fill up the stewpan with as much liquid as you need jelly.

Add *if necessary* some one colorant. Let the whole simmer for three or four hours, then strain through a fine strainer & when cold carefully remove every particle of fat.

When cold to clarify the jelly, beat up the whites of two eggs in a sauce pan, half melt the jelly, pour it in & keep stirring on the fire till it boils a few minutes. Add a wine-glassful of taragon vinegar & strain thro' a flannel jelly bag, if necessary strain a second time, the jelly should be clear as unclouded amber—

A. L. D. H. to S. A. D.
S. D. Fair Haven Sept. 1879

[*A. L. D. H. to S. A. D.—Annie Lyman Delano Hitch, Sara Delano's older sister, who married Frederick Delano Hitch, to Sarah Alvey Delano. S. D.—Sara Delano.*]

Laplanders*

1 quart milk
1 quart flour
2 eggs
1 teaspoonful of salt
a small lump of butter

Heat the pans before putting in the batter and bake in the oven—
Laplander pans can be had at all hardware shops.

S. D. from Mrs. J. T. Johnston
Plainfield, June 6th, 1879

[*S. D.—Sara Delano. Miss Delano visited the Johnstons in Plainfield from June 3 to June 6, 1879.*]

Beef Tea

Take a pound of lean beef, free from fat and separated from the bone. Chop it as fine as mince-meat. Pour upon it a pint of cold water & let it stand for 2 or 3 hours & then bring it slowly to a boil. After boiling briskly for a minute or two, strain the liquid through a fine sieve, & add a little salt—The same plan may be adopted with mutton or chicken.

Mrs. Carey to A. L. D.

[*Mrs. Carey was the mother of Sara Delano's girlhood friend, Maggie Carey.*]

* An asterisk following the title indicates a reference to this recipe in the Notes for Cooks following the Household Book.

Soft Waffles

1 lb. flour	¼ lb. butter
4 eggs	1 quart of milk

2 tablespoonsful of yeast & let them rise. Sugar & cinnamon after they are buttered if you like.

S. A. D. to S. D.

[*S. A. D. to S. D.—Sarah Alvey Delano to Sara Delano.*]

Oyster Soup

Two quarts of oysters, strain off the water thereof, then boil it, add pepper & ~~salt~~ water as much as is wanted. Take 6 or 8 crackers soaked in half water & half milk for thickening. When the water is boiling, add the crackers mixture & let it boil up once.

Then throw in the oysters & let them boil up once, just as you take them off, add a little piece of butter.

Fair Haven—Turkey Soup*

Boil up the old carcase bones, stuffing & all, add a little rice, pepper, salt, & onion (the latter fine). The stuffing must go in last say 20 minutes before taking up.

Catsup is a good condiment to add—

A hearty soup.

Mrs. Sturgis—Receipt for Curry

Warm 4 oz. fresh butter to a liquid, then fry six large onions, sliced, nearly brown. Take a tablespoonful of curry powder, 3 cloves of fresh garlic & an inch length of green ginger, mashed, & well mixed with the curry powder & about 2 spoonfuls of cold water. Cast this into the pan with the already browned onions, cover it & keep shaking the pan over the fire till the spattering noise ceases, then put in either your fowl, cut up as for a stew (beef, mutton or lamb not exceeding 2 pounds) & stir the whole for ten minutes until partially brown— After this add a pint of boiling water and set the pot on to simmer until tender enough to serve.

Curry powder

Mrs. Sturgis

8 oz. Turmeric
1 oz. Green ginger
4 oz. Coriander seed
2 oz. Black pepper
4 oz. Cummin seed
½ oz. Cardamum seed
½ oz. Powdered mace
1 oz. Cayenne pepper

[*Dr. and Mrs. Russell Sturgis of Boston were good friends of the Roosevelts, and also went to Campobello in the summer.*]

Bouillon

Take 4 pounds of juicy beef from the round (if not to be served as bouillon better cut it in pieces & crack the bone.)

Put it into a stewpan or stock-pot & pour in 5 pints of cold water, one pint for each pound & one over, half a spoonful of salt to help the scum rise.

Put the pot on the fire with the cover on & let it come quickly to the boil. Add a little cold water & skin it well.

Add four young carrots cut small, one onion, 2 leeks, ½ head of celery, & let simmer gently for five hours. Watch & skin it occasionally. Once or twice more add a little cold water to raise the scum.

Take a cloth & put over an earthen basin, & a hand sieve over the basin, pour the contents into the sieve & through the cloth, into the bowl. Put into a cool place until the next day & carefully remove all fat. Stir thoroughly into the soft jelly the whites & shells of two eggs. Put on the fire & boil 10 or 15 minutes. Strain through a fine sieve or cloth into a tureen & serve.

This makes enough for a lunch party of 12.

Mrs. Ward's receipt.

[*The Wards were friends of the Delanos. Mrs. Ward was the mother of Sara Delano's friend Marian Ward Low.*]

To Boil Rice

Wash half a pound of rice in salt & water & put it in 5 pints of boiling water if Carolina rice—boil 20 minutes. drain it in a cullender & set it near the fire to dry.

Shake it into a dish without touching it.

Méringues*

Springle some sugar on them before baking

Beat up the whites of four eggs, then put in half a pound of powdered sugar & mix well into the egg. Then with a silver spoon put a spoonfuls on in rows on strips of white paper & lay the papers on thin board in the oven. The oven must not be hot, but must bake them slowly for half an hour. After dropping them off the paper, take out the soft inside & put them on their backs into the oven for a few minutes to dry.

Harriet Wood's receipt.
S. D. Fair Haven, Sept. 1879

[*S. D.—Sara Delano.*]

Bavaroise*

Dissolve half a box of Cox's Gelatine in a pint of milk. Whip a large coffee cup full of thick sweet cream & strain the gelatine into it, put in also sugar & vanila extract, to suit the taste.

Whip the whole together, put it into a form, & place it in the refrigerator to cool.

Algonac receipt.

Puffs—Rosa Mulligan*

1 pint flour—1 pint milk
1 tablespoonful sugar, a little salt
4 eggs, a lump of butter the size of an egg & a half.

Proceed thus:

Put the sugar & salt into the flour, mix in the milk little by little, make *smooth,* then the eggs & beat well, about 2 minutes & add the melted butter.

Grease pans, bake slowly ¾ of an hour.

[*Rosa Mulligan was the cook at Algonac from 1873 to 1880.*]

Broth receipt

—from Dr. Ely
Jan. 16th, 1880

1 lb. of beef or mutton, cut up fine taking out all the fat. Add a pint of cold water, let it stand two hours, let it simmer 15 minutes, strain, put it away in a cold place, then take off all the fat that rises. Then heat up.

[*Dr. Smith Ely of Newburgh was the Delano family physician.*]

Harriet Wood's receipt for Beef tea

2 lbs. lean beef in a pint & a half of cold water, soak 2 hours, with a little salt. Then boil in a sauce pan ¼ hour, skim it, and let it get cold into a clear jelly.

Calf's head

After scalding, cut & take out brains, then soak till white
& clean, close it & tie in a floured cloth & simmer till it
[seems] *quite* tender, so that a fork will stick in easily. When
sufficiently tender spread open on a tin (skin side out),
cover over with beat up egg, scatter over it pepper, salt,
bread crumbs & finely chopped parsley & a few bits of butter
here & there, then brown in the oven. Make a batter of the
brains, make fritters & garnish the dish. If any left, take off
the bones & make a fricassee or hash for lunch. Boil the feet
tender till the bones slip out, let them get cold, & when ready
to cook, let them simmer till they are hot, & dip in batter
& fry, or hash them.

from Harriet Wood
Feb. 12th, 1880

Gingerbread*

    1 spoonful good beef dripping
1½ cup of molasses
    1 cup buttermilk
    2 teaspoonfuls of ginger
A little salt & a teaspoonful of saleratus, make as thick as
pound cake with flour & beat for three minutes.

from Harriet Wood
February, 1880

Strawberry preserves

Strawberries & crushed sugar, pound for pound. Put the sugar on them over night & in the morning put all into the preserving kettle & after it comes to a boil, boil for ¾ of an hour, taking off the scum as it rises with a *silver* spoon. Stir *gently* with a *wooden* spoon.—Then dip up the strawberries into the glass jars & the surplus juice can be strained & put into bottles for flavoring ice cream etc.—

Currant jelly

String the currants, put them in the kettle, let them boil 20 minutes. Take them off & strain them in a cloth into a bowl. To a pint of juice a pound of sugar (heating the sugar first & stirring the hot sugar into the juice) let it come to one good boil, then fill the glasses.

Mrs. Jewett's receipt
received from Mother Roosevelt
Hyde Park, July, 1882

[*Mrs. Jewett was a family friend of the John A. Roosevelts and Mrs. Dr. Isaac Roosevelt—Mother Roosevelt.*]

Very strong Chicken & Beef Tea
for an invalid

Take all the skin & fat off an old hen, cut it up & joint it, cut up a pound of lean beef stripped of all fat & skin, put both in a stone jar with a pint of water and a little salt & a blade of mace put on a cover or cork with a cloth under it tied down to keep in the steam; boil six hours in a pot of water; strain it off; when cool take off the fat leaving a clear jelly.

A wine glass full three times a day is enough.

From Harriet Wood
Algonac, September, 1882

Mushroom Catsup

 1 peck fresh mushrooms
½ pound of salt
   Let stand 2 or 3 days.
To each quart of mushroom liquor ¼ oz. of cayenne,
½ oz. alspice
½ oz. ginger
 2 blades pounded

Put all in a stone jar in a saucepan of water, let it boil three hours. After it is cold, bottle it & take care to exclude the sediment. Add a few drops of brandy to each bottle & seal it.

from Harriet Wood   1882

Pickled Onions

Peel the onions with a silver knife, taking off two skins.
Place in the dry bottles
Cover with vinegar, to each quart of it put
2 teaspoonfuls of alspice
2   "   whole black pepper
Will be ready to use in two or three weeks & keep good 6 to
8 months.

H. W.   1882

[*H. W.—Harriet Wood.*]

Soup of green pea shoots*

Plant green peas in a box or pots in the greenhouse & use
the young shoots for a purée when only a few inches high.

(Sir Hugh L. H. Cholmeley
"Easton", Grantham. 1885)

[*Sir Hugh and Lady Cholmeley were friends of Mr. James Roosevelt;
he had known them many years before his second marriage.*]

Maryland Biscuit*

3 qts. flour
4 tablespoonfuls lard
1½ pts milk
1 teaspoonful yeast powder

Sift the yeast powder with the flour, then rub in the lard thoroughly & add one teaspoonful of salt & the milk. Work into a stiff dough & beat half an hour.

Bake 20 or 25 minutes.

From J. W. D. Mt. Savage, Sept. 1880

[*J. W. D.—Jennie Walters Delano, Mrs. Warren Delano III, sister-in-law of Sara Roosevelt. Mt. Savage, Maryland—the Walters country place.*]

Asparagus Soup*

Select about 2 dozen good asparagus stalks, boil them thoroughly in enough water to cover them & add a quarter of an onion. When tender take the asparagus out of the water & saving the water, remove the onion, cut the asparagus into small pieces, of course only the tender part & put them in a mortar, adding a little of the water. They must be pounded until perfectly smooth. Now take some sifted flour a dessertspoonful, a bit of butter as large as an egg & a very little powdered sugar. Mix well & then put on the fire until it ~~boils~~ melts, stirring all the time.

This add to the pounded asparagus & the rest of the water. When it has boiled a few minutes mix the yolk of an egg with a tumberful of cream & add this. If properly made it wants no straining. Use salt & pepper to the taste & a very little nutmeg. One stalk of asparagus may be left which can be cut in thin slices & added last.

From J. W. D.   Mount Savage
Sept. 1880

[*J. W. D.—Jennie Walters Delano, Mrs. Warren Delano III, sister-in-law of Mrs. Roosevelt.*]

Raspberry Vinegar

Put the raspberries into a stone pot, cover them with vinegar and let stand three or four days stirring several times a day. Strain through a double cheese cloth, then put a pound of juice to a pound of sugar and let it come to a boil then bottle it—boil 15 minutes & remove scum.

From Mrs. Jewett, Rosedale
July, 1883

10 quarts raspberries
2   "   vinegar

[*Mrs. Jewett—friend of Mrs. Dr. Isaac Roosevelt, Sara Roosevelt's mother-in-law.*]

Veal Loaf*

3 lbs. tender veal chopped fine
3 eggs—6 crackers rolled
2 teaspoonsful of cream
1   "   "   salt
1 oz. thyme or parsley
1 oz. blk. pepper

Mince well & bake in loaf shape 1½ to 2 hours basting while cooking with butter & water.

From J. W. D. 1880

[*J. W. D.—Jennie Walters Delano, Mrs. Warren Delano III, sister-in-law of Sara Roosevelt.*]

Veal Pie*

Take part of a hind quarter of veal with all of the bone & let it boil about six or eight hours.
Boil four eggs hard.
Make your pastry & put inside your veal with the liquid & the hard boiled eggs, season to taste.

J. W. D.   1880
Mount Savage

[*J. W. D.—Jennie Walters Delano, Mrs. Warren Delano III, Mrs. Roosevelt's sister-in-law.*]

Pork & Beans*

Beans to be well washed & put in cold water & boiled for two hours with only enough water to boil themselves dry.
The pork to be boiled in a separate pot, but when tender to be put with the beans for half an hour, just previously to their being done. The beans after boiling to be seasoned with salt & pepper & a little sugar or molasses is better then put in a baking dish, the pork in the centre of the beans & put in the oven to brown.

From E. M. C. R. Rosedale
December, 1883

[*E. M. C. R.—Ellen Murray Crosby Roosevelt, Mrs. John A. Roosevelt, sister-in-law of Sara Roosevelt. Rosedale was the name of the John A. Roosevelt residence.*]

Wafers for Tea*

Two or three tablespoonfuls of flour, & milk enough to make a very thin batter.

A piece of butter the size of a walnut, drop a teaspoonful of the batter on the iron. Heat the iron, then butter it or grease it with a piece of salt pork.

From Lilly Ellison—1884

[*Miss Ellison was a Newburgh friend of the Delanos. She was present at the Delano-Roosevelt wedding.*]

Welsh rarebit*

Fresh white fine cheese cut in half inch blocks, put in a bit of butter in the chafing dish then the cheese which you stir until it is the consistency of molasses, then add a tablespoonful of beer, keep stirring, add five mustard spoonfuls to ~~each~~ every three people, add two more tablespoonfuls of beer, one at a time, & add one third of a tablespoonful of red & black pepper mixed.—

From Mrs. James Lawrence—1883
Campobello—

[*Mrs. James Lawrence of Groton, Massachusetts, was a friend of the Roosevelts who often spent the summer at Campobello.*]

Currant Cordial*

1 lb. currants—(*white* if you have them) picked clean
1 oz. Ginger bruised
1 oz. bitter Almonds
1 oz. sweet Almonds
1 oz. sweet almonds
1 quart whiskey or rum

All to remain covered 48 hours then strain through a linen towel—To every quart of juice add one pint of clarified sugar. To one lb. of sugar, one pint of cold water and boil till clear, then mix & bottle—

Fish-Balls*

1. Pint bowl of the raw codfish after it has been flaked.
2. pints of whole potatoes or if large in halves.

Put the raw potatoes into a large sauce-pan full of water &
throw the fish on top. Boil 25 minutes, then drain off the
water & shake up the potatoes & fish in the pan.

Mash it until light, adding a *little* cayenne pepper, & one
or two eggs (first well beaten) also a lump of butter *half*
the size of an egg.

Have the lard *boiling* & drop in the balls shaped in a tablespoon.

Two minutes will suffice to fry one. Take out and place
on some brown paper in the open oven to drain.

A D H   from Miss Parloa's book
Algonac—May 5th, 1885

[*This recipe is in Mrs. Hitch's handwriting. A. D. H.—Annie Delano
Hitch. Miss Parloa's book was entitled* Maria Parloa's New Cook Book
and was published in 1884.]

Gingersnaps*

1 pint of molasses
½ pint of sugar
2 cups of Butter
1 cup of water
2 tablespoonfuls of ginger & a little salt.
1½ tablespoonfuls of dry saleratus (water measure) stirred in the molasses. Add flour enough to make the dough very stiff.—

(N. F. C.

Sugar cookies

2 cups of sugar	Beat sugar &
1 cup of butter	butter
1 cup of milk	together

2 teaspoonfuls of dry saleratus stirred in the milk, a little salt, and flour enough so that the dough can be rolled. Add the caraway seeds when the dough is nearly mixed.

(N. F. C.

[*N. F. C.—Nancy F. Church, Sara Delano Roosevelt's "Cousin Nannie," who lived with the Delanos at Algonac for the last twenty years of her life.*]

Mint Sauce

2 tablespoonfuls of green mint cut fine, add
2 tablespoonsful of sugar
~~½ a teaspoonful of vinegar~~
½ a tea-cup full of vinegar

(A. L. D. H.)

[*A. L. D. H.—Annie Lyman Delano Hitch.*]

Thin biscuit for tea or after cheese

Lay on the Paste board one pound of flour & a little salt, mix
with ¼ of a pound of butter, adding a small quantity of milk
& kneading as for bread. Then roll very thin & cut into
biscuits.
Bake in a moderate oven.

A. D. H.
Algonac, May, 1885

[*A. D. H.—Annie Delano Hitch.*]

Oyster Toast

Bruise two anchovies fine in a mortar.
Take one dozen oysters & cut them up, put the anchovies &
oysters into a small saucepan, mix with them sufficient cream
to give it a pleasing consistency. Heat well over the fire,
stirring it all the time, spread it on rounds of buttered toast
& serve it up *hot*.

A. D. H. Given her by Mr. Charlesworth

(Eat it in solemn silence & wash down with a glass of brown
sherry or cherry brandy.)

[*A. D. H.—Annie Delano Hitch.*]

Barley Broth (Gerteschleim)

Put whole barley for a minute in a little butter on the range
to soften it, then boil it in soup for three hours & strain it
thro' a sieve.

(Kissingen. August 1884.)

Raspberry Water ice*

4 quarts of raspberries squeezed thro' a cloth
3½ coffee cups of granulated sugar
1 pint of water

Beaten up until the sugar melts, then put in a freezer &
after well freezing it pack tightly for 2 or 3 hours.

(Rosa. Algonac. 1885)

[*Rosa—presumably Rosa Mulligan, the cook who left Algonac in
1880.*]

Devonshire Cream

1 pailful of morning's milk in a deep pan *or* stone jar let it
stand 12 hours or in cold weather 24 hours, then put the pan
on the stove & let the milk get so hot that little bubbles come
in the centre but not all over, then take it off *quickly,* let
it stand 12 hours in the dairy.

(Mrs. Bennett, St. Leonards on Sea
November, 1884)

[*Mrs. Bennett, St. Leonards-on-Sea, England—unidentified.*]

Devonshire Pudding*

from Bessie Simes
Tunbridge Wells, March, 1885

2 oz. bread crumbs
2 oz. butter
½ pint of milk & 1 teaspoonful sugar. Mix & put them in a saucepan & stir till boiling. After boiling a minute or two take it off & let it cool. Add two eggs well beaten. Butter a pie dish & put in the mixture. Bake about 20 minutes, & turn out on a flat dish. Put on a layer of good jam & some whipped cream over all.

[*Bessie Simes—cook?*]

Ginger Pudding*

½ lb. flour
¼ lb. suet
¼ lb. moist sugar
2 large teaspoonfuls of grated ginger

Shred the suet very fine mix it with the flour, sugar & ginger, stir all well together, butter a basin & put the mixture in *dry*. Tie a cloth over & boil for 3 hours. Have a bowl to hold the above pressed in tight & let the above ingredients be exact quantities.

(Bessie Simes)
Tunbridge Wells, 1885)

Rum or Wine Jelly*

For each quart of water one pkg. of gelatine—in summer a little more.

1 quart water
3 lemons (juice & peel (*no* white rind).
1 large cup sugar
3 little pieces cinnamon

Put all in a bowl in the evening & in the morning boil it in a saucepan adding white of two eggs to clear it (for 2 quarts of water 3 whites of egg), boil till it is sticky when tried with a spoon, then pass this thro' a sieve & a flannel, & freeze in a pan with a little rock salt & ice. *Add the rum* or wine when ready to freeze *not* while hot.

From Julie Weiss, cook
November, 1885

Apple Bavarois*

Peel & cut up a saucepan full of apples with very little water to moisten them. Add 1½ cups of sugar & a pkg. of gelatine, cook it all well & then pass it thro' a sieve. When it is cold mix with it ½ pint of whipped cream, well mixed put in a form & freeze with a little salt & ice.—

Julie Weiss. Nov. 1885

Preserved Strawberries

1 lb. strawberries to
¾ lb. of granulated sugar.

Put in layers in the preserving kettle & *boil* for 20 minutes.
Then fill the glass jars quite full & refil as they settle. Seal
after the preserves are cold.

From Lilly Ellison
Algonac, June, 1886

[*Miss Ellison was a family friend of the Delanos, from Newburgh.*]

Strawberry ice-cream

1 quart of strawberries
1 pint of sugar
   Mash together & let stand two or three hours
Add one quart of cream
Strain through a cullender then whip it up a little & freeze
it.

Algonac, June, 1886

Whortleberry griddle cakes*
as made in Fair Haven

½ cup of sugar
 1 heaping tablespoonful of butter
 2 eggs
 1 pint of milk
A little salt
Flour enough to make a nice batter.
Stir in a pint of berries at the last & fry the cakes on a griddle
quickly

Squash Pie*

(Mother Roosevelt's recipe)

 1 quart of squash all strained
 1 pint of milk
 1   "   "   cream
 6 eggs
 1 piece of butter the size of an egg warmed & put in the
   squash
 1 heaping tablespoonful of ginger
 1 teaspoonful of cinnamon, a little salt—
Beat together, put it warm in the paste—

[*Mother Roosevelt was Mrs. Dr. Isaac Roosevelt, Sara Roosevelt's
mother-in-law.*]

J. R.'s receipt for egg-nog

Put a little powdered sugar into a tumbler
A teaspoonful or more of brandy
The yolk of an egg
½ a tumblerful of milk,

then fill up with cracked ice not too fine & shake well together in a shaker (a big tin tumbler & a strong glass tumbler)
Strain it into a clean tumbler & put on top a suspicion of nutmeg.

[*J. R.—James Roosevelt.*]

To detect an escape of sewer gas
in the house

Take an ounce of oil of peppermint & pour it down the ventilating pipe.—If you smell it anywhere in the house, there is an escape of sewer gas.

Receipt for a cough

—from Miss Riggs—Washington

½ lb. rock candy
1 pint whisky *or Jamaica rum*

Pound the candy & put in a quart bottle, pouring the Jamaica rum over the candy.
Place the bottle (lightly corked) in a sauce pan of hot water and let it remain on the edge of the range until the candy is dissolved.

March, 1887

[*Miss Riggs—unidentified. Perhaps a trained nurse?*]

Preserved strawberries

To each lb. of fruit 1 lb. of sugar
Fruit & sugar in thin layers not more than 4 lbs. of fruit at
one boiling, set on a slow fire till melted then after it boils
let it go on boiling 25 minutes, skimming all the time. Then
take the berries out on a meat dish & let the juice boil into
a syrup, then put the berries back & let the whole thing
come to one good boil, when it will be finished.

From Mrs. Archie Rogers
June 20th, 1888

[*Mrs. Archie Rogers—friend and Hyde Park neighbor of the James
Roosevelts.*]

Buckwheat cakes*

(Kassie. Dec./88)

Scald 2 *tablespoonsful* of Indian meal in 1 pint of boiling
water.
Add 2 *cupsful* of buckwheat flour &
1 tablespoonful of yeast
Let this stand over night.
In the morning add
⅓ teaspoonful saleratus desolved in a little water.
½ teaspoonful of salt
1 tablespoonful of molasses.
This must be a thin batter—& fried on a griddle in boiling
lard.

[*Kassie—Mrs. Roosevelt's younger sister, at that time Mrs. Charles A.
Robbins.*]

To clarify sugar

To 3 lbs. sugar
1 pint water & the white of 1 egg.
Beat well [with?] ½ pint water, when it boils up & the scum
rises, take it off the fire, set it by till it falls, then take the
scum off.

from E. M. C. R.

[*E. M. C. R.—Ellen Murray Crosby Roosevelt, Mrs. John A. Roosevelt,
Sara Roosevelt's sister-in-law.*]

Cornbread*

1 pint milk
1 cup indian meal
2 tablespoonfuls of flour
2 eggs
A little salt
1 tablespoonful melted butter
1 large teaspoonful royal baking powder.
1 tablespoonful of sugar.
Bake on jelly plates in a moderate oven, very thin.

(Algonac)

Another very good & cheap

1 pint milk
1 cup cornmeal
2 tablespoonfuls flour
A little salt
A tablespoonful of sugar
A table " "   Royal Baking powder

Molasses pudding*

    1 quart of milk
    3 eggs beaten up
    1 teaspoonful cinnamon
    1   "   ginger
    1½ cups of molasses

Cut bread thin, butter it & lay in layers, soak for an hour.

from Mrs. James Lawrence

[*Mrs. Lawrence came from Groton, Massachusetts, and was a Campobello friend.*]

Wine whey for invalids

Boil the milk, then pour in the wine & when the curd gathers, strain it twice.
    1 pint milk
    ½ tumbler of sherry.

To preserve tomatoes*

Pour boiling water on the tomatoes to loosen the skins, peal & put the tomatoes into the preserving kettle, when hot add two handfuls of salt, boil for an hour or *two* if very juicy. Stir with a wooden spoon, frequently. Make the jars *very* hot & fill with the boiling liquid quite to the brim & screw on the top with rubber band at once. When cool tighten as much as possible.
If you preserve okra with tomatoes for soup put half of each, cutting okra very thin.

(Algonac)

Ginger snaps*

1 cup sugar
1 " butter
1 third of molasses
1 half of sour milk or cream
1 teaspoonful of saleratus
1 tablespoonful of ginger
Flour enough to roll,

roll very thin & bake quickly.
Care must be taken not to mix too much flour in the dough.

Café Mousse*

One large cup of black coffee
Yolks of 6 eggs, beaten light with 1½ cups of granulated sugar. To this add coffee & return to the saucepan & cook until thick & put away to cool.
1 quart of cream, whip & take off till all is whipped. Then take the whipped cream put it in a large bowl, to this add the coffee custard stirred in gently, put immediately in the form which must be already packed in ice & salt. Shut tightly & leave 3½ or 4 hours.

From E. M. C. R.
"Rosedale"

[E. M. C. R.—*Ellen Murray Crosby Roosevelt, Mrs. John A. Roosevelt, Sara Roosevelt's sister-in-law. Rosedale was the John A. Roosevelt residence in Hyde Park.*]

Méringues*

1 cup granulated sugar
Whites of 4 eggs
Whipped separately & baked about 20 minutes on a board.

E. M. C. R.
"Rosedale"

[E. M. C. R.—*Ellen Murray Crosby Roosevelt, Mrs. John A. Roosevelt, Sara Roosevelt's sister-in-law.*]

Calf's head & liver*

Soak the head over night, split it in halves.
Boil in very little water to *partly* cover, with carrots, celery, onions, & parsley. Boil about 2 hours, strains off the juice & remove the bones.
Put butter in a frying pan to brown with a little flour, when brown, add some of the soup, with finely chopped onion & two small pickled cucumbers chopped fine.
Cut the liver in small pieces & fry in another pan in butter until brown, then put in the sauce & cook for a half hour. Fifteen minutes before serving, add the cut up calf's head with a little salt & cayenne pepper. Put in a good sized glass-full of wine, sherry or port, just before dishing.

Algonac, Nov. 2nd, 1891

Maryland chicken

Disjoint the chicken, fry in a pan with a good big lump of butter, adding salt & pepper.
When fried, put the chicken on a hot platter & stir into the melted brown butter remaining in the pan, a cup of fresh cream, & perhaps a little more salt & pepper. Let this sauce be well heated through again & then pour it over the chicken & serve.

Mont Blanc*

Peal the chestnuts, put them into cold water & on the fire. When cooked take off any remaining skins, put them back into a saucepan with a little butter & mash them. Add a little sugar, milk & a very little vanilla & cook a little longer. Strain through a sieve, on to the dish when cold & put whipped cream around it.

Pau. January, 1890

Brandy Peaches*

Peel the fruit carefully with a sharp silver fruit knife, drop the peaches into cold water as you peel them.
Put the peaches into boiling water a layer at a time, as they become tender, take out one by one with a spoon & lay on a tray with several thicknesses of white cloth or towelling. Cover with a cloth to keep them white while draining.
Fill your jars with the fruit, then turn in a small teacup or less of granulated sugar, & *fill* the jars with brandy.
Screw your covers on tight. Next day tighten again & put the jars bottom side up.
Turn them until all the sugar has melted into the juice.

(Algonac. A. D. H. 1891)

[*A. D. H.—Annie Delano Hitch.*]

Cough mixture

⅔ Jamaica rum
⅓ Glycerine
1 teaspoonful whenever the cough is troublesome.

Gargle for sore throat

A teaspoonful of chlorate of potash, 2 teaspoonfuls of common salt, 20 drops of carbolic acid to one pint of water

from Mrs. Alfred Pell
1897

[*Mrs. Alfred Pell lived at Highland Falls, near Newburgh, and was an old friend of Mrs. James Roosevelt.*]

Moonshines

1 quart flour
½ ~~1 heaping~~ teaspoonful salt
2 tablespoonful butter, 1 cup cold water
~~½-1 tablespoonful lard~~
  mixed & stirred dry
~~Then add slowly~~
~~1 egg beaten up in a cup & filled up with milk~~
Mix well & roll out *very* thin a *little at a time.*
Cut out in rounds and bake in a hot oven about 5 minutes.

~~from Anne Reynolds cook~~
~~1884~~

1 quart flour   ⎫
1 teaspoon salt   ⎬ mix and stir dry
¼ lb. butter   ⎭
1 cup cold water
roll the dough as thin as possible into squares or circles,
bake 5 minutes in hot oven.

Clam broth*

Wash the clams thoroughly in two or three waters, then
put them on the range in a saucepan, *nearly* covered with
water. The Clams will open & the juice mixes with the
water. *Strain* out the clams & add a *little* pepper.

Indian Chutney

4 quarts pared, cored, & sliced tart apples
4 quarts green tomatoes, chopped fine
2 lbs. stoned raisins, chopped fine
3 onions   "   "
3 pints brown sugar
1½ pints lemon juice
3 pints vinegar
2 gills salt
2 teaspoonsful cayenne pepper
2 tablespoonsful powdered ginger

Put all in a stone pot, let stand overnight. In the morning place jar in kettle of cold water, after coming to a boil, boil 6 hours stirring occasionally— Heat pint Mason jars & cover while hot.

from A. D. H.

[*A. D. H.—Annie Delano Hitch.*]

Pan Dowdy*

Pare & quarter apples & put them in a brown earthenware
crock.
Add 1 cup of molasses
1 tablespoonful of cinamon
a little sugar & water enough to moisten.
Cover with cream of tartar paste. Bake slowly from 2 to 3
hours, then break the paste in & serve cold.

from Mrs. James Lawrence
Groton

Lobster à la Newburg*

1 pint cream   }
Yolks of 3 eggs   } beaten up together
2 tablespoonsful brandy
2   "   sherry
A little red pepper & salt
2 table spoonfuls of butter

Proceed thus:

Put 2 spoonfuls butter in a frying pan, when melted, put in the lobster which sh^d be cut into small pieces, heat it, then add the wine, & brandy & seasoning. When thoroughly hot stir in the cream & eggs.

Mushrooms*

A lump of butter less than the size of an egg. Add cream & a little milk & salt, let it get hot, then add the mushrooms, also a *little* cornstarch. Salt the mushrooms well, pepper a little when nearly done. Cook about 20 minutes.

From Mrs. Sturgis
Campobello /94

[*Mrs. Russell Sturgis of Boston, a Campobello friend.*]

Finnon haddie

First cut the fish lengthwise in two parts, skin & take out the backbone, fins, etc.

Place upon a baking dish with a little butter & water.

Sprinkle *lightly* with flour & pepper, add a little milk & cook in a hot oven for five minutes.

"Teutonic" 1895

[*The* Teutonic *was a steamship of the White Star Line, on which the Roosevelts made several crossings to Europe.*]

To stew dried fruit

Soak the fruit all night in luke warm water— Make a syrup and cook the fruit in it till it is soft.

From a German lady

To cook "Nouilles" or macaroni*

Boil thoroughly, add salt, then butter & finely grated cheese, one may add "sauce tomate"

Bake very slightly in oven.

Curry

Letitia Hayward's receipt
Very good

Warm 2 or 3 oz. fresh butter to a liquid.

Fry 3 large onions sliced, *nearly* brown, also a sliced apple & the red of 2 carrots.

½ tablespoonful of curry powder, a little garlic & ginger & salt ~~pieces of apple.~~ Cook the meat ~~a little of the red part of carrot, a very little water~~ till tender then cast it ~~all this to be well mixed together~~ & cast into the pan with the browned onions, etc.

Cover the pan & shake it well over the fire until the sputtering noise ceases, then put in the meat & stir the whole for ten minutes.

Add if the meat is fresh ½ a pint of boiling water, if the meat has been cooked, add some stock instead of water, then let it simmer until tender enough to serve.

Serve only boiled rice with curry—

[*Letitia Hayward was a cook in the house at Hyde Park from January 1903 to July 1904.*]

Pan Dowdy—2nd receipt

Line a "baked bean pot" with paste, fill it with apples peeled & quartered.

Add a small bowl of brown sugar, one cup of molasses, one teaspoonful ground cinnamon.

One teaspoonful of ground alspice, one cup of water.

Cover with paste & bake in a slow oven for 3 hours—

Stir in the crust, bake again slowly until the crust is absorbed.

From Miss Parker
(Staatsburgh)

[*Miss Parker is not positively identified, but might have been Miss Alice Parker, niece of Mr. and Mrs. Henry Parkman.*]

Tea Cake

Take bread dough enough to make a loaf of bread.

Work into it six eggs (or less) the yolks only, ½ cup sugar.

2 tablespoons of butter—Work thoroughly & raise for 2 hours.

Put in tins the size of a saucer shape of large buns & bake in a medium oven 15 minutes—butter well on the top & sprinkle with cinamon & sugar *or* almonds & sugar.

Spice Cake*

from Mrs. Alfred Pell

1 cup butter
2 cups sugar
3 eggs whites & yolks beaten together
3 cups flour
1 cup milk
½ teaspoonful soda
heaping   "   cream of tartar
1   "   nutmeg
¼   "   cloves
¼   "   allspice
heaping   "   cinamon
½   "   ginger
1 cup raisins
1   "   currants

[Mrs. Alfred Pell of Highland Falls, near Newburgh, a close friend of the Roosevelts, with whom Mrs. Roosevelt and Franklin went abroad in the summer of 1901.]

Cornbread

receipt from Wm. Yapp, porter on D & H. car
he calls it egg bread

½ pint of milk, bring to a boil, & stir in until it is smooth
 1 teacup full indian meal
 1 large tablespoon of lard
½   "   " butter
A little salt—stir well all the time, when cool add about
 2 *tablespoons* of flour,
1 teaspoon of baking powder then beat in 3 eggs.
beat it up, grease the pan, pour in an *inch* deep—bake 15
 minutes in a quick oven.

To Cook Baker's cracked cocoa

Steep thoroughly in water 2 cups of cracked cocoa in a cocoa pot (porcelain lined) covered with 3 quarts of cold water, set it on the back of the range, let it come to a boil & simmer for at least four hours. It can be filled up with water several times & when it gets too weak, turn out the grounds & start fresh. Can be kept on the stove night & day but it is better not to really boil, only to *simmer,* boiling makes it bitter.

Very good served with hot milk & cream like coffee.

from Mrs. H. S. Russell
Milton

[*Mrs. Russell was a friend of Mrs. Roosevelt who lived at Milton, New York, a little north of Newburgh.*]

Zwiebach

Algonac
May 1905

Take about 2 quarts of regular bread dough in the morning.
Add
      1 cup butter
      1 " sugar
let it all raise as for any biscuit.
After baking them allow them to become cold— Split with
a steel knife & place in a slow oven to bake for half an hour
until brown.

Then place on the heater on top of the range to become
crisp & dry.

To cook a ham

Soak over night if Ferris, 36 hours if Smithfield or Tod. First wash & scrub. Put in ham boiler in cold water with generous soup greens & 2 stalks of celery.

Place with skin down & let simmer until the ham turns over of its own accord. Take out & skin while hot.

Trim it & cover it with coffee a. sugar. Take one bottle of cooking sherry put ham in a baking pan and baste for one hour with the sherry.

Use cider if preferred *or* champagne

Adirondack dessert

Make large *thin* pancakes butter each & spread with granulated maple sugar, pile one on the other.

From M. Low
July, 1905

[*M. Low—Marian Low, Mrs. Abbot A. Low, close friend of Mrs. Roosevelt.*]

Clear soup

Any bones you have *or* a soup bone say ½ a shin—Cover
with water.

boil for one hour. Add your vegetables, carrotts, onions,
cabbage, turnips, celery, etc. boil for 2 hours. Put through a
cullender, let all stand all night—skim in the morning, clear
with 2 eggs or shells & whites of 4 or 5 eggs & ½ lb. of beef
stirred all together.

let it simmer on back of range for an hour till it comes
to a boil, then boil for an hour.

Strain through a cloth and let it cool.

Dish made of boiled fish*

Pick the fish carefully, put the cooked spinach in the dish
a layer of it, then a layer of fish, seasoned with salt & pepper.
Make a béchamel sauce by boiling the fish bones & skin,
strain it. A tablespoonful of flour,
                "   "   " cream
                "   "   " butter
making ½ or ¾ pint of liquid. Pour that over the fish, grate
cheese on top, bake in the oven. This can be made with
highly seasoned mashed potatoes.

Crullers

2 lbs. flour
10 oz. sugar
6 oz. butter
7 eggs
1 nutmeg
A *little* rose water
Roll them out quite thin & cut with jigging iron like sample paper.

Tea cake

Take bread dough enough to make a loaf of bread. Work into it 6 eggs.

see page 79 [186]

Grape fruit ice

Shred grape fruit & squeeze it
add sugar & freeze

Sauce for it

Juice of 3 oranges & 3 lemons,
a little sherry & rum, boil it a little & let it get cold—

Fish Salad

Any good cold fish, cod or halibut.
Remove all skin & bones, soak while hot with vinegar for
one hour on ice. Mayonnaise and a teaspoonful of finely
chopped onion & 1 tablespoonful of capers—chopped cucumbers or pickles, all mixed in the mayonnaise & a little red
pepper—

Luncheon dish

½ chicken & ½ ham minced & mixed with 1 tablespoon-
ful celery salt *or* chopped celery—
2 tablespoonfuls of cream.
Make a large sized pancake, fill in centre & roll up tight.
Put in oven & serve with Hollandaise sauce.
Smelts may also be used as filling.

Oatmeal cakes

  1 cup Quaker or other oats
¾ cup of brown sugar
¼ cup " butter
  1 egg
  1 teaspoonful baking powder

Mix butter & sugar together, then the egg & then the oats
with the baking powder—
Drop on baking sheet with a teaspoon—

Cup Cake

(Mrs. J. A. Weekes)

			2 for small families
4 cups	flour		
1	"	butter	½
3	"	sugar	1
1	"	milk	½
5 eggs			3

1 teaspoonful soda disolved in milk
2 teaspoonfuls cream tartar mixed in flour
(in small family ½ teaspoon of soda & less than 1 teaspoon
of cream tartar.

Beat the butter & sugar into a cream, add yolks of eggs,
beat well again.

Then add the milk with the soda in it, beat again, then
add flour with the cream of tartar in it, beat again, put in
whites of eggs, lastly add teaspoonful lemon extract & bake
quickly in very hot oven in well buttered tins.

[*Mrs. J. A. Weekes, a cousin of Mrs. Roosevelt, was Alice Delano
before her marriage. Mr. and Mrs. John A. Weekes were present at
the Delano-Roosevelt wedding.*]

Mince meat

best receipt

2½ lbs. currants
2½ " raisins
2½ " brown sugar
2½ " beef suet
2½ " greening apples & the rind & juice of 2 lemons
  1 teaspoonful of salt
  1 lb. mixed candied peel, (lemon, citron & orange)
  1 teaspoonful each of *ground* cinnamon, alspice, ginger,
    mace
  ½ teaspoonful cloves, (ground)
  1 tablespoonful grated nutmeg
  1 pint good sherry
  ½ " " brandy

chop the suet, raisins, apples, and candied peel *fine,* mix all
thoroughly, put in a stone jar & stir frequently to let the
moisture be evenly [distributed] through the whole mixture

from Mrs. O'Callaghan
English cook
June 1907

[*Mrs. O'Callaghan is not further known to fame.*]

Entrée dish for lunch*

Make puff paste, roll very thin, put the oysters on the range to get hot in their own liquid, set them away to grow cold & dry. Season with salt & pepper, put one or two oysters in a piece of puff paste & roll it up, closing the edges tight, roll that in egg & bread crumbs, fry in boiling fat, then place in oven to get *very* hot. Can be served with any sauce.

New England Brown Bread

(from A. D. H.)

¾ cup of molasses
2 "   " rye meal
1 "   " indian meal
1 "   " flour
1½ pints milk
A little salt
1 teaspoonful (water measure) bi-carbonate of soda.
1 egg well beaten

Boil for 4 hours steadily.
This will fill a 5 lb. lard tin. Secure the cover with a cloth tied on & let it get cold, if necessary to slice for toast.

[*A. D. H.—Annie Delano Hitch.*]

Minute pudding

1 pint of milk
2 even tablespoonfuls flour
2 eggs

Scald milk—[Put] flour in bowl
Break eggs into bowl
Beat a few minutes, then add the scalded milk.
Cook five minutes in a double boiler.
When taking off fire add a pinch of salt.

Sauce

Boil ½ cup of molasses 20 minutes, serve both very hot.

Sicilian Sherbert

(*from Ellen*)

1 can of peaches or apricots, cut in small pieces, *or*
1 quart of fresh peaches
Juice of 3 oranges.
3 tablespoonfuls of lemon juice.
1 cup of sugar.
Mix & freeze.

[*Ellen might have been Mrs. John A. Roosevelt, or her daughter,
Sara Roosevelt's niece.*]

Cranberry Punch

1 quart of cranberries
2 cups " water
1½ " " sugar
juice of 3 oranges
1 tablespoon of mareschino

freeze & serve with whipped cream & cherries. Boil berries till tender, press thro' a sieve, add sugar & orange juice. Cool about 20 minutes & freeze.

Gooseberry Jam

Clean the berries.
To one lb. of berries allow one lb. of sugar—
Cover the berries with water (not too much) & boil half an hour *or* long enough for the berries to fall to pieces.
Stir occasionally to keep from burning as they burn easily. Remove from range & put in jars or tumblers. This is more a *preserve* than a jam.

(from E. W. D. Adams.)
1908

[*E. W. D. Adams—Ellen Warren Delano Adams, Mrs. Frederick Adams, daughter of Warren Delano III; Mrs. Roosevelt's niece.*]

Maitre d'Hotel butter

½ cup butter
 1 tablespoon lemon juice
½ teaspoonful salt
 1 tablespoonful chopped parsley
½ saltspoon pepper

Cream the butter & add the seasoning, stirring it well.

Hollandaise sauce

½ cup butter   1½ tablespf. of lemon juice.
 1 saltspoonf. salt   ⅓ cup boiling water
¼   "   cayenne
Yolk of 4 eggs.

Cream the butter, stir in yolks of eggs unbeaten *one at a time,* beat well, add the seasoning & beat with a Dover beater, for five minutes—add the boiling water, set the bowl in a saucepan of boiling water & beat till it stiffens—remove *immediately* when done, or it will curdle.

Preserved Rhubarb

Scald the rhubarb after cutting in 1 inch pieces, let it drain. Put it on the range in a preserving kettle & let it simmer & when it begins to be juicy add one cup of sugar to a quart of fruit. Then cook it for 15 minutes fill the jars to overflow, & seal hot—

Fromage à la crême

Keep 2 or 3 quarts of milk, till it is curdled, drip it thro' a cheese cloth until all the water (or liquid) is out.

Pass the rest thro' a sieve & beat it up with fresh cream, pour it into a mould lined with cheese cloth, let it stand two hours— Unmould it & pour fresh cream over it.

To make the milk turn quickly, put it on the side of the range to warm it a bit.

From Fay—(Paris)

[*Fay—Miss Fay Forbes, sister-in-law of Mrs. Paul Forbes (Dora Delano), Mrs. Roosevelt's older sister.*]

Gooseberry "Kräm"

Stew gooseberries with a little water not to boil long. Add one piece of cinamon—thicken with a little potato flour, & then boil a little longer.

(Swedish way)

Thin biscuits*

2 cups of flour
1 tablespoonful & a half of butter mixed with the flour &
½ a teaspoonful of salt.
2 tablespoonsful of baking powder

Mix all together with a little water lightly with a fork. Sprinkle flour on a board, & roll gently till about ½ an inch thick, then cut with a biscuit cutter.

The same sort of dough *thicker* for strawberry shortcake or *any* shortcake.

To cook cereal for Anna and James

1909

Oatmeal—
2 heaping cups of H. O. soak in cold water for ½ an hour, & boil in double boiler 2 hours.

Granum
1½ cups—mix with cold water to a paste—let it stand ½ an hour before cooking—

Cream of wheat
1 cup to a quart of water, soak as you do granum.

Wheatena—
1 cup & 3 teaspoonsful to a quart of water.
  Boil all cereal 4 hours.

[*Anna and James—two older children of Franklin D. Roosevelt; Mrs. James Roosevelt's grandchildren.*]

Wheat bran muffins*

    1 pint wheat bran
    ½ cup   "   flour
    ½ "   graham "
    Mix together and add ½ pint milk
    2 tablespoonsful molasses
       then add
    1 teaspoonful baking soda
    ½ "   soda
    ½ "   salt
    bake in small tins

Devonshire cream

    4 quarts milk, set for 12 hours (covered) say from 6 P.M.
till 10 A.M.
    Then set on the back of the range & allowed to almost
~~boil~~ come to a boil, when the first little bubbles come on it
Then set again in the same pan for 6 hours & skim.

from Mrs. Philip Martineau

[*Mrs. Philip Martineau's husband was a cousin of Cyril Martineau.
Mrs. Roosevelt's younger sister Kassie's daughter Muriel married
Mr. Cyril Martineau.*]

Risotto*

Mince an onion, put it into a 3 quart saucepan & brown it with 3 oz. butter.

Take out the onion—put in 1 lb. rice & ½ a glass of Marsala.

Reduce over a quick fire, add 1 quart of stock, boil hard so as to reduce in 18 minutes—

Take it off the fire, season with 1 oz. of butter

    1 oz. grated parmesan cheese

    3 or 4 fowls livers & mushrooms, minced up fine & a little good gravy—serve hot

Scotch short bread *

¼ lb. butter

2 oz. sugar (powdered)

6 oz. flour

2 oz. rice flour, *or* cornmeal *or* semolina *or* potato flour

knead on a slab, working in the flour—

Toffy

½ lb. fresh butter
 1 " brown sugar
 1 teacupful cream *or* milk
 1 tablespoonful *molasses*
 1 teaspoonful of lemon juice to be added *after it is cooked*

To be boiled 25 or 30 minutes stirring all the time—

Calves Head

Cooked like terrapin—from Lily Waldron—

good in chafing dish

Mash the yolks of 6 hardboiled eggs, with 2 heaping tablespoonsful of butter, mix till perfectly smooth—

Add one pint of the liquor the calf's head was boiled in, mix in salt & black & red pepper to taste.

Place on the range & cook 5 minutes. Add a bowl of calf's head & the whites of the hard boiled eggs cut in pieces as large as a five cent piece— Serve very hot & add just before serving a half cup of good sherry—This is

[*Lily Waldron has not been identified.*]

Barley Water

Squeeze 2 lemons, *peel* & *juice*
1 teacup of pearl barley a *little* sugar
2 quarts of boiling water

Let it stand until it cools then strain it—

Forest Lodge—Hythe
August—1912

[*Forest Lodge, Hythe, England, was the home of Mrs. Cyril Marti-*
neau (Muriel Robbins), Mrs. Roosevelt's niece.]

Quince Honey

5 large Quinces peeled and grated.
4 pounds of sugar and 1 pint of water boiled until sugar
melts.
Add the quinces and boil slowly ten minutes.
This will keep in glasses like jelly without being sealed.

[*Page pasted in, not in Mrs. Roosevelt's handwriting.*]

Candied orange peel

Cut the peel of 6 thick skinned oranges, into straws. cook in water well salted until soft enough to pierce with a silver fork without breaking. Make a syrup of sufficient sugar & water to almost cover the amount of orange peel & cook until the peel has taken up the syrup. Lay out on a plate well covered with granulated sugar & roll each piece separately in the sugar, laying aside in another plate. The peel should be rolled again in fresh sugar, which when left over can easily be used in cooking or other preserves. Orange peel burns easily and after it begins to take up the syrup, should be stirred with a fork, taking care not to break the straws.

(Nice for table decorations with bon-bons).

[*Page pasted in, not in Mrs. Roosevelt's handwriting.*]

A D H 's receipt for raspberry Vinegar

10 quarts of raspberries
2   "   " cider vinegar—

Let it stand in a stone crock three or four days at least, stirring frequently. Squeeze thro' a double cheese cloth— To each pint of juice add one pound of sugar & boil 15 minutes, removing the scum while boiling. When cold bottle & seal.

[*A. D. H.—Annie Delano Hitch.*]

Water glass—made of Sillicate of Soda— to preserve eggs—

Heat eight quarts of pure filtered water & let it boil twenty minutes. Pour into a large pan. When luke warm, stir into it one quart of full strength solution of Sillicate of Soda.

Pack your eggs carefully in a stone crock and cover with the solution when cold.

When the jar is full, cover with a strong white cloth & then the jar cover. Keep the [jar] in the coolest place in the house, if you have not a cold room.

from A D H —August 1914

[*A. D. H.—Annie Delano Hitch.*]

Loganberry punch

1 quart Loganberry
1 pint gingerale
1   "   sparkling water.
Juice of 6 lemons
  "   " 5 oranges
1 orange cut in five slices & quartered
& about a cupful of syrup—(melted sugar)

from E. B.
1918

[*E. B.—Eleanor Blodgett, a close friend of Mrs. Roosevelt, and Franklin D. Roosevelt's godmother.*]

Ham in Jelly

from E. M. C. R.

Boil the ham— Any that is left, put a tablespoonful of butter & half a glass of currant jelly in a pan. Lay some slices of ham cut very thin into the mixture and bring it to a boil.

Professor Nash's receipt

[*Professor Nash has not been identified. E. M. C. R. was Ellen Murray Crosby Roosevelt, Mrs. Roosevelt's sister-in-law.*]

Canada's War Cake

2 cups brown sugar
2   "   hot water
2 tablespoons lard
1 teaspoon cinnamon
1   "   salt
1   "   cloves
1 package sultana raisins
Boil all these ingredients 5 minutes after they begin to bubble. When cold add:
3 cups flour
1 teaspoon soda, dissolved in 1 teaspoon hot water.
Bake in two loaves, 45 minutes in a slow oven
This cake is better at the end of a week—

Apple sauce Cake*

½ cup butter
1 " sugar
½ " molasses
2 " apple sauce
1 teaspoon ground cloves
1 " " cinamon
½ " ginger
½ " soda stirred into a little water
3 cups flour—a pinch of salt

Curry

Warm two tablespoonfuls of butter to a liquid.

Slice 4 large onions & fry in the butter to a light brown.

Cast in pieces of chicken (1 chicken) having taken out bones & skin—

When the chicken is a little brown, put the whole thing into a cooking pan, & put in the sauce,

Sauce

4 or 6 onions (fried)
1 spoonful of flour—
1 tablespoonful curry powder
1 sliced carrot, 1 sliced apple—
1 teaspoonful of salt
1 pint of hot water *or* stock.

Cover it & cook it slowly & let it simmer until tender—

In using *cooked* egg or meat or vegetable, omit the flour & put the sauce thro' a *sieve*.

Grape fruit marmalade

1 grape fruit
1 orange
1 lemon—
Slice all thin *or* put through a meat chopper.
Add 3 quarts of water—
Let stand 24 hours—
Then boil 1½ hours—
Let stand another 24 hours.
Then add 5 lbs. sugar, & cook slowly until thick, which will be about 1½ to 2 hours.
Remove core, seeds & tough sections before grinding.
This will make *about* 12 glasses.

Currant Conserve

5 lbs. currants
5 " sugar
1 pkg. seeded raisins cut small
Yellow rind & juice *of 4 oranges*

Cut off the orange peel of 4 oranges & put in a small sauce pan of cold water— As soon as it boils pour off the water & cover again with cold water, let that come to a boil & pour off.

The peel will be soft & in small pieces to be cooked with the currants & sugar until all are ready for the small jars.

from A. D. H.

[*A. D. H.—Annie Delano Hitch.*]

Corn Bread—without eggs or butter—

1 cup warm milk
½　"　white corn meal
A pinch of salt & a teaspoonful of Royal Baking Powder.

　Add the salt to the cornmeal, then pour in the warm milk & mix—
　Turn into shallow pan not more than ¼ of an inch thick
　Bake in a moderate oven until crisp—

Baked bananas

　Take a strip off top, put little bits of butter along the bananas & bake about 15 minutes.

Devonshire Cream

　Let a pan of new milk stand for 24 hours—do not skim but place it over a very slow fire and gradually bring to *scalding* not to boil. The cream will thicken on the surface & should be *not* disturbed for 12 or 14 hours. It sh^d be cold when taken off.

Fruit Punch*

Receipt from Una

Put a lump of ice in the pitcher—Then:
1 bottle sparkling white grape juice
1 bottle gingerale
1 pt. white rock
juice of two oranges
    "   "   "   lemons
sweetening to taste
Some crushed mint
slice 2 oranges in the pitcher & a little banana & cucumber,
if you wish. Mix just before using & stir well.

[*Una—a Roosevelt cousin, the daughter of Mr. James Russell Soley.
Miss Soley later became Mrs. Charles M. Connfelt.*]

Indian Pudding

(for 6 or 8 persons)

2 cups beef suet (finely chopped
1 " molasses
1 " brown sugar
3 yolks of eggs
1 cup Indian meal
1 " bread crumbs
1 " milk
1 teaspoonful baking soda, dissolved in hot water
1½ to 2 cups raisins
1 pinch of salt

Butter a mould & steam for 3 hours.
Serve with hard sauce

Moonshines

1 quart of flour
1 cup of cold water—to be added to mixture which is stirred *dry*
¼ lb. butter
½ teaspoonful salt—

Mix into a dough & roll as thin as possible. Cut into squares or circles, a few at a time & bake in the oven 5 to 10 minutes.

To Cook Swiss Chard

Cook a *little* & throw out the water—
Then put bits of salt pork into it & cook all together with
hardly any water & add a little salt when finished—& serve.

Spanish Rice

1 cup rice
2   "   cold water
1 teaspoon salt
boil 20 minutes—

A large piece of butter in frying pan
A large onion & a red or green pepper finely chopped—
When cooked add the rice & mix all thoroughly

Economical Corn Bread

One Cup warm milk
Half Cup white corn meal
Pinch of salt, teaspoonful of Royal Baking Powder

Add salt to corn meal and pour in the warm milk and mix.
Then turn into a shallow pan to the depth of one fourth of
an inch.
Bake in a moderate oven until crisp.

[Printed recipe, pasted in. "Economical" was written in in pencil.]

Currant Jelly

String the currants, put them in a kettle & boil them 20
minutes—
Take them off & strain them in a cloth into a bowl— To
a pint of juice, a pound of sugar, *heat* the sugar first & stir
the *hot* sugar into the juice. Let it come to *one* good boil.

[Pasted in.]

Excellent hair wash

2/5 pure alchohol
2/5 " olive oil
1/5 best perfume, violet or jasmine—

Put in bottle, shake well rub a little in with fingers & brush well.

Remedy for seasickness

½ a little flat bottle of liquid mercury—worn over the "solar plexus"—

Child's Stocking

Cast on 52 stitches—
Rib one, purl one for 10 rows—
Knit 60 plain rows—
narrow 4 times with 5 rows between.
Knit 40 rows & divide as in regular sock for heal
Turn the heel & knit 40 rows to where you narrow for toe—

—Paquebot "Paris"—

LES CRÊPES
"C'est Paris"

"Seul l'homme c
sait manger.
BRILLAT-SAVARI

[*Pasted in.*]

RECETTE
pour 10 Crêpes "C'est Paris"

Frotter sur l'écorce d'une orange 4 morceaux de sucre, r
sur l'écorce d'une citron, 2 morceaux de sucre, écraser
sucre dans le jus d'une demie orange et y ajouter la valeur
80 grammes de beurre.

Mettre ce beurre préparé dans un plat, faire chauffer, bien
étendre les crêpes, les retourner, les plier en quatre et les
saupoudrer de sucre cristallisé. Les arroser ensuite avec les
liqueurs suivantes, que l'on aura eu soin de mélanger à
l'avance:

> Un verre à liqueur de Rhum
> Une verre à liqueur de Bénédictine
> Un verre à liqueur de Cointreau
> Deux verres à liqueur de Grand Marnier

Pencher légèrement le plat de façon à faire enflammer les
liqueurs, retourner les crêpes pour qu'elles soient bien im-
prégnées de la saveur du mélange, servir bien chaud, et
vous aurez ainsi tout le secret des crêpes
"C'EST PARIS"

Le Maître d'Hôtel

[*Printed leaflet.*]

RECIPE
for 10 "Paris" Pan-Cakes

Rub 4 lumps of sugar on the peel of an orange, then 2 lumps of sugar on the peel of a lemon, crushing the same lumps of sugar in the juice of half an orange and add to the same 80 grammes of butter.

Place this prepared butter in a pan, heat the same, spreading well the pan-cakes, turn them over, fold in four, and powder with cristallized sugar.

Afterwards sprinkle the cakes with the following liquors, which should be mixed in advance:

> One liquor glass of Rum
> One liquor glass of Benedictine
> One liquor glass of Cointreau
> Two liquor glasses of Grand Marnier

Tilt the frying-pan in such a way, so as to ignite the liquors, turn the cakes over, so that they will be well saturated with the flavour of the mixture, serve them very hot, and then you possess the secret of making "PARIS" Pan-Cakes.

The Chief Steward

[*Printed leaflet.*]

Helmet

Set up 20 stitches & knit 30 rows—
Take up side stitches on second needle knit back & take up other side stitches on third needle making 80 stitches in all, which knit back & forth for 32 rows.
Add 12 stitches in front to connect sides under chin, put on 3 needles, & knit 3 purl 3 round & round for 3 inches— Then divide the stitches in half, one being front the other back. Knit front 46 inches back & forth on 2 needles 34 rows & bind off. Now knit the back half on two needles back & forth for 30 rows & bind off. Take up stitches around face & knit 3, purl 3 for 9 rounds & bind off.

Improve land—Crimson Clover

sow 12 or 13 lbs. to the acre, can also sow it on a corn field on last cultivation of corn.

For *Cherry trees*. Ground bone & nitrate of potash—10 lbs. of *each* around a large tree— Spray early with Paris green—

For *Peach trees*—3 or 4 lbs. potash & bone around each tree —spray with arsenate of lead—

To finish toe of stocking

Set stitches on 2 needles

Nearest needle.
   Take of first stitch as if to knit put needle thro' 2nd stitch as if to purl but do not take it off.

Farthest needle
   Put needle thro' first stitch as if to purl & pull it off. Put it thro' 2nd stitch as if to knit & do not take it off—& repeat—

Knitted Sponge

Dexter cotton—No. 6. Needles size 7
Cast on 41 stitches very loosely; knit 14 rows over & back; bind off *very* loosely, dropping every other stitch.

(New England Branch Am. Fund for for French Wounded.)
306 Boylston St. *Boston*

Formula to help *laying* hens

60 lbs. corn meal
30 " bran
60 " middlings
50 " meat scraps
10 " alfafa meal
10 " oil meal
 5 " salt—

Mix well & feed during the cold months.—

Receipt for pot pourri

from Mrs. Griswold

2 oz. ginger root
6 oz. bruised alspice
3 oz. stick cinnamon
2 oz. bruised cloves
3 oz. bruised nutmegs
1 oz.   "   anise seed
20 grains true musk
1 lb. fresh lavender flowers
4 oz. bruised orris root
1 dram oil of jasmin
1   "   "   "   rose geranium
1   "   "   "   lavender flowers
1   "   "   "   lemon
A few drops each of oils of Verbena
violet, Neroly & Patchouly—
One bushel of fresh roses

(the leaves)—Put them in a large covered jar, in the following way. To every 3 handfuls of rose leaves, 1 handful of salt. Allow them to remain for 10 days, stirring every day. Then add all the spices & perfumes & keep well covered—Fresh leaves may be add to this stock each year—

[*Mrs. Clifford M. Griswold, née Norah Brewer, wife of one of the popular masters at Groton, from 1892 to 1936.*]

For rheumatism

Oil of gautheria (checkerberry) for *external* use (from Mrs. John Gray—)
buy at Melvin & Badger—Temple Place, Boston

Pink liquid powder
9. 12. 524326
Hass Pharmacy—

[*Mrs. John Gray—not identified.*]

Nurse Watson often gave Baby Anna for breakfast
oatmeal—she boiled it thoroughly till it was very soft, then
strained it and added a little *salt* and it became when cold
a good jelly—Anna ate it with milk poured over it—quite
a bowl full—& drank two cups full of milk, well warmed—

1907

[*Baby Anna—oldest child of Franklin D. Roosevelt.*]

Malaria Cure

from W. D., Jr.
August 1908

12 powders—each to have 20 grains Calcined Magnesia
40 grains Peruvian Bark

Take one powder each day before breakfast in a tumbler of water for 12 consecutive days—

[*W. D.—Warren Delano III, Mrs. Roosevelt's brother.*]

Child's Jersey

4 needles.   Begin at neck

64 stitches rib 2 & 2 for 1½ inches or 2 inches
At each side knit plain 7 or 8 across 3 inches for shoulder.

Then take up stitches of neck & shoulder pieces & knit across back & front about 16 stitches, back & forth.
Then knit round & round until the jersey is long enough, & rib at the bottom about 2 inches. Pick up stitches for sleeves, knit round & round & rib at the wrists.

Baby jacket

crocheted in 3 threaded saxony

A chain of 100—crochet 24 & in the 25th stitch widen by putting 2 stitches in one hole—do the same in the 27th stitch. Then crochet & widen in the 27th and 25th from the other end. Widen every row always over the one commenced until 8 double rows are made, crocheted by taking up back stitch —Begin with 2 *threaded saxony* in treble crochet 4 trebles in every other stitch of the yoke, make chain of 28 stitches from front of yoke to back for sleeve, across fronts of yoke there should be 17 shells each & 31 shells across back of yoke —21 rows of white, then 3 of colour, then 3 of white. Crochet a border down between the shells of split zephyr, the same shade as the yoke—

Sleeves—Crochet 19 shells, say 7 across yoke & 12 across chain, make 14 rows of shells. Crochet band by putting *one* in each stitch of single crochet. Four rows of colour, then a row of white shells & border of colour down between the shells.

Neck—Make a row of treble crochet in color for a ribbon —then a row of white shells & a border of color going down between the shells—

from E. M. C. R.

[*E. M. C. R.—Ellen Murray Crosby Roosevelt, Mrs. John A. Roosevelt, Sara Roosevelt's sister-in-law.*]

For hard wood floors

When already waxed & polished, they need to be daily wiped with a broom with a canton flannel cover tied over it— Also to rub frequently with a piece of good quality burlap, boil the burlap for an hour or two, then cut in squares & bind with tape.

For common hard wood (pine) floors *or* oilcloth
rub twice a year with raw linseed oil 3/5
turpentine 2/5 well shaken up—

Baby socks

Cast on 28 stitches
Widen 3   "   each row at one end then narrow for the toe at the other until 26 stitches are left, then widen every other row until you have 32. Then cast off 14 slip and bind, knit 3 pearl plain, then cast on 14 stitches and narrow at the toe every other row until 26 are left, then widen every row till there are 31, narrow for the heel, leaving 28 stitches. Take up the stitches for leg, widen once in two stitches, knit 3 pearls of white then put in color—½ oz. of white ¼ oz. of colour.

From N. F. C.
Algonac 1878

[*N. F. C.—Nancy F. Church, Cousin Nannie.*]

Give Chickens in winter to encourage them to lay eggs:

Warm water three times a day in their drinking troughs.
A little Pratt's poultry food—
All the carcases of chickens & turkeys & soup meat left in the kitchen.
Dried leaves to scratch in—throw a little wheat & corn in among the leaves—

For a cough or cold, keep a saucepan of water steaming over an etna *or* kerosine stove in the room, pouring into the water a teaspoonful, (to a quart of water) of creosote—
It is soothing & disinfecting.

Beechwood Creosote—
¼ lb. bottles (Hartman and Bauers) sold by Merck & Co. N. Y. Can be had at any chemist's.

Cheap & good Roofing paint

1 gallon "coal oil" (crude petroleum) $2 to 2.50 per single barrel.
4 lbs. rosin
2½ " Prince's Metallic paint

Mix the Petroleum and the Prince's Metallic. Then melt the rosin & pour it into the mixture stirring until thoroughly incorporated.
Costs about 17¢ per gallon.

from W. D. Jr.

[*W. D. Jr.—Warren Delano III, Mrs. Roosevelt's brother.*]

Very good cold cream

(Dr. Satterlee's prescription)

424.25) at Hegeman and Co.
196 Broadway

[*A family of Satterlees lived in New Hamburg, Dutchess County, with whom the Roosevelts were very good friends. Dr. Satterlee may possibly have been of this family.*]

Gargle for *sore throat*

½ bicarbonate of soda
½ salycilate of soda
well mixed—½ a teaspoonful in ½ a glass of water

Warm sontag of germantown
single zephyr—

40 stitches
Knit 42 purls, then put on 40 more stitches & knit 42 more
purls
take off 40 stitches & leave them on an extra needle & after
knitting 42 more purls, bind off together with the 40 stitches.

[*A "Sontag" was a knitted or crocheted cape with long ends which
tied behind at the waist. This garment was named for Henriette Sontag, the German singer.*]

Sore Throat remedy

1 teaspoonful glycerine
½   "   chloride of Iron
½ a glass of water
Gargle & take one teaspoonful every 2 hours.

(from Miss Dreyer, Mama's trained nurse 1887)

Also

4 spoons molasses
2   "   olive oil
1   "   paragoric
1 teaspoonful when needed.

Spasmodic or Membranous croup

Solution of bicarbonate of soda (one teasponful in a tumbler
of water), & a 16th part of a teaspoonful of powdered Ipicac
stirred in the solution.
Give a teaspoonful every 10 or 15 minutes.

Dr. Parker

[*Dr. Parker was the same Dr. E. H. Parker of Poughkeepsie, who
brought Franklin Roosevelt into the world.*]

Furniture Polish

1/3 sweet oil
1/3 vinegar
1/3 alcohol

To freshen crape—

Ring out a blk. cloth in water & spread it over the crape
flat on the table, then go over it without pressing *at all* with
a hot iron—

How to Wash Silk Knit Articles

Wash in lukewarm water, using a very little white castile
soap in the water (no other), and avoid rubbing the article
as much as possible.

Rinse in clean, cold water, and squeeze the article in a
clean, dry cloth to dry it. Never wring it; never use acid or
alkali in washing silk. Dry at once, and when dry, place between a dry, smooth cloth with weight enough to press the
article smooth, after which take a soft, dry flannel cloth and
rub lightly, which will give a finish to the silk.

Always use HEMINWAY'S KNITTING SILK, WHICH IS PURE SILK
AND PURE DYE.

[*Above three paragraphs printed and pasted in.*]

Peña handkerchiefs should be washed in cold water and
never in hot—

For Sprains

Instead of bandaging paint every 24 hours with *"Contractile Collodium"*.

If necessary to wash it off use ether for it— Do not paint too often as it would produce a swelling the same as too tight bandaging—

Mustard Plaster

1 heaping dessert spoonful mustard
8 dessertspoonfuls flour.
Mix with the white of one egg, adding enough water to make it the right consistency.

(Kassie)

[*Kassie—Mrs. Roosevelt's younger sister, who married first Charles A. Robbins, and then H. Price Collier.*]

For Croup

Alum & Honey
1/3 powdered alum
2/3 honey—

Diarrhea in an infant

A teaspoonful ful of lime water in a little milk *or* flour, drops of paragoric in a little water.

When older a little boiled milk or toast water or rice water, sometimes a teaspoonful of castor oil is needed with a little paragoric.

Constipation

A Castile soap suppository or 2 teaspoonsful of Olive oil.

Wind

Catnip or Camomile tea—

Thrush

Borax & honey on a brush to wash the ~~mouth~~ & to take a few drops several times a day of the following
    5 grains Chlorate of Potash in
    4 tablespoonsfuls of water

Mrs. Lee

[Mrs. Carrie Lee, the trained nurse who attended Mrs. Roosevelt when Franklin was born.]

Arrowroot

1 teaspoonful of arrowroot to a cup of milk— When the milk is boiling, mix the arrowroot with a little water to form a smooth paste, put it into the milk stirring it carefully for a few minutes to prevent any lumps. Take it from the fire & add a little salt & if the child likes, a little sugar.

Wheat gruel

Tie ½ pint of flour into a cloth & boil it 3 or 4 hours— Then dry the lump & grate it when you use it—Then make a thin paste of the flour with water & add to milk & boil it.

Treatment of Croup

(Dr. Parker)

A child under a year—¼ teaspoonful syrup of Ipicacuenha to be repeated in 20 minutes if no vomiting occurs previously. When free vomiting has been produced ½ the quantity will suffice.

A child 2 years old may have ½ a teaspoonful full every 20 minutes until it vomits & so on with its increasing years.

[*Dr. Parker was the physician who attended Mrs. Roosevelt at Franklin's birth.*]

For Fever blisters

Subnitrate of Bismuth applied dry on blister.—

Diarrhea Mixture

For a child 18 months old one teaspoonful full every two hours or at longer intervals of the following mixture.

    3 oz. chalk mixture
    ½ oz. tincture of Kina (or catechu.)
    ½ oz. compound tincture of cardamoins.

Shake the bottle well. Good for simple diarrhea.

For a cold

in an infant a couple of months old *syrup of Tolu*
    ¼ of a teaspoonful every 3 or 4 hours in a teaspoonful of water. A child over 3 or 4 months may take of *Syrup of ipecacuanha* 3 to 5 drops in a teaspoonful of water once in 3 to 4 hours. After 6 months 5 to 10 drops may be given & after the 18 months to 2 years ¼ to ½ a teaspoonful. After a child is 2 years old a little *Brown Mixture* is good.

For Cankers—Marsh rosemary

Cough Syrup

Steep thoroughwort or boneset, strain it, add molasses
enough to make a syrup, boil down—
Add a pinch of senna.
To *keep it,* add whiskey.

For cleaning black stuffs

½ oz. of borax
½ oz. of camphor, add half a pint of boiling water & later
again ½ a pint of boiling water.

List for layette from Marian Low

1881

(Mrs. Abbot A. Low)

12 night slips
12 simple dresses
 4 day flannel peticoats
 4 night "　　　"
 3 or 4 dozen small diapers
 3 or 4　"　large　"
12 white peticoats
12 pair of socks
　　fine flannel to tear into Bands
12 aprons to hold rubber cloth
 3 flannel aprons for nurse
 6 knit shirts
 6 pillow cases
 6 crib sheets
 2 mattress covers

Pour compter
il faut 40
semaines ou
280 jours commençant
plusieurs jours après
l'indisposition

Notes for Cooks

Notes for Cooks

MANY of the recipes in the Household Book date from the days when no exact and accurate system of cooking measurements was in use. Further, Mrs. Roosevelt was not herself an experienced cook, and, having mentioned basic ingredients, often left details such as seasonings and methods of preparation to be worked out by the person who did the cooking.

In order to help readers achieve better results with some of the delicious dishes Mrs. Roosevelt thought worth recording, a few suggestions and amplifications are offered. These are taken almost entirely from Maria Parloa's *New Cook Book,* 1884, and Fannie Farmer's *Boston Cooking School Cook Book* (Little, Brown and Co.)

Warning: The authors of the Household Book are but amateur cooks, and have not scientifically kitchen-tested Mrs. Roosevelt's recipes.

LAPLANDERS, p. 142

Laplanders are the equivalent of our present-day popovers. Better results will be achieved if the ingredients of Mrs. Johnston's recipe are cut down to:

1 cup flour	2 eggs
7/8 cup milk	1 tablespoon melted butter
1/4 teaspoon salt	

Beat ingredients until well blended—about 2 minutes. Fill pans only 1/3 full of batter.

Popover or Laplander pans should be of iron and should be buttered or oiled and heated for 10 minutes in a 450° oven before putting in the batter. Bake for 20 minutes in a 450° oven, then reduce heat to 350° for 15 minutes.

SOFT WAFFLES (RAISED WAFFLES), p. 143

Aunt Sarah Alvey Delano's recipe was based on the idea that every household, like the Delanos', numbered ten to fourteen or more at mealtime. More reasonable amounts are given by Miss Parloa as follows:

"1 pint milk	1 teaspoon salt
1½ pints flour	¼ yeast cake or ¼ cup liquid yeast
1 egg	

If yeast cake is used, dissolve it in 2 tablespoons cold water. Have milk heated to 98° (blood-warm) and add to it the yeast, salt, and egg, well beaten. Stir gradually into flour. Cover and let rise four hours. Bake on waffle iron."

TURKEY SOUP, p. 143

The best modern advice on this says to omit the stuffing. Use 6 cups of water to an average carcass; boil for one hour; then add ½ teaspoon salt, ¼ teaspoon paprika, ½ cup onion, and 3 tablespoons barley instead of rice, and simmer for another hour. One cup carrots and 1 cup celery with leaves, added for the second hour, will give more flavor (and more vitamins) than the older recipe.

MERINGUES, p. 146

Harriet Wood suggested a silver spoon from which to drop beaten egg whites and sugar on white paper. The recipe will be more efficacious if no particular attention is paid to the kind of metal in the spoon, but if the board she refers to is wet before the white paper is laid on it. Give these 15 minutes in a 250° oven.

BAVAROISE, p. 147

Today's measurements for this rich and tasty dessert:

1 tablespoon gelatin soaked in 2 tablespoons cold water
1¾ cups scalded milk
1/3 to ½ cup sugar
½ teaspoon salt
1½ teaspoons vanilla
2 cups whipped cream

Add sugar and salt to the scalded milk, and stir in the gelatin. As the mixture thickens, add the vanilla and beat with a wire whisk. When the pudding is fluffy, fold in the whipped cream. The pudding form should be wet.

ROSA MULLIGAN'S PUFFS, p. 147

This pastry does not fall into the category of puff paste, nor is it easy to translate into twentieth-century terms. It might be best to avoid meddling, and to say simply that butter the size of an egg usually means about one-quarter of a cup, and butter the size of an egg and a half would equal one-third of a cup.

GINGERBREAD, p. 149

For 1 cup buttermilk and 1½ cups molasses, 2¼ cups flour will make this gingerbread "as thick as pound cake." One-half teaspoon of salt would do for "a little salt." Saleratus, of course, is bicarbonate of soda.

Bake about 25 minutes at 350°.

SOUP OF GREEN PEA SHOOTS, p. 152

Sir Hugh did not go far enough with this recipe. Miss Parloa offers the following:

"Cover a quart of green peas [or shoots] with hot water and boil, with an onion until they will mash easily. (The time will depend on the age of the peas, but will be from twenty to thirty minutes.) Mash, and add a pint of stock or water. Cook together two tablespoonsful of butter and one of flour until smooth, but not brown. Add to the peas, and then add a cupful of cream and one of milk. Season with salt and pepper and let boil up once. Strain and serve. A cupful of whipped cream added the last moment is an improvement."

MARYLAND BISCUIT (BEATEN BISCUIT), p. 153

The "yeast powder" to which Mrs. Delano refers is baking powder. The lard should be chilled, as well as the milk. And beating half an hour means about 200 strokes with a mallet, or until the dough is well blistered. These biscuits call for a 325° oven.

ASPARAGUS SOUP, p. 154

Butter the size of an egg is a quarter of a cup, and a dessertspoon of flour is a tablespoon. A tumblerful of cream may be translated as a standard measuring cupful.

VEAL LOAF, p. 155

The amount of spice to be added to three pounds of veal in this recipe seems excessive, whereas according to the rule of 1 teaspoon of salt to every pound of meat, there is not enough of that commodity. Three teaspoons salt, 1 teaspoon black pepper, and one of parsley or thyme probably will be more satisfactory than the quantities given.

VEAL PIE, p. 156

This recipe needs considerable amplification. The direction to "take part of a hind quarter of veal with all of the bone," may be freely translated to "take a knuckle of veal" and simmer in water to cover until meat is tender (about 3 hours). Remove meat, cut in small pieces, mix with three or four minced hard-boiled eggs, add a bit of bay leaf, a sprig of parsley, a slice of onion, all minced fine. Moisten with the stock in which the veal was cooked. Instead of making a pastry cover for this, today's cooks may wish to bake in a casserole with a biscuit-dough cover, until meat is heated through again and cover is brown—about 15 minutes at 400°.

PORK AND BEANS, p. 156

From the length of boiling time given, Mrs. John A. Roosevelt must have meant kidney beans, not the pea beans usually associated with this dish. Three tablespoons sugar to a quart of beans is about right for seasoning, although those cooks who agree with Mrs. Roosevelt that molasses is better will need to add about 2 tablespoons of that ingredient. Presumably the pork to be used is fresh.

WELSH RAREBIT, p. 157

Fannie Farmer puts this recipe on a more businesslike basis. She says:
"1 tablespoon butter   ½ teaspoon mustard
½ lb. soft, milk cheese cut in small   1/3 to ½ cup ale or
   pieces—few grains cayenne   lager beer
¼ teaspoon salt
1 egg slightly beaten
Melt butter and add cheese and seasonings. As cheese melts add ale or beer gradually, stirring constantly, then egg. Serves 4."

CURRANT CORDIAL, p. 158

This recipe brings up the question of the alcoholic beverages served at Springwood. As a child, Mrs. Roosevelt had been accustomed to seeing wines served at table, not only when she was abroad, but at Algonac. An unidentified newspaper clipping (1879) surviving from the Algonac days discourses on the subject as follows: "For dinner parties or private dinners where wine is used with the different courses it is as well to have on the table light claret, still hock, still Moselle or white Bordeaux; these wines are put in small decanters between the covers and have to be replaced when empty. Champagne is served with oysters; Madeira or sherry with soup; sparkling hock or Moselle with fish; with the releves Bordeaux; with the cold entrees a kind of hock. 'Pour couper le dîner' as the French say, it is usual to give a glass of Roman punch. With the cheese some old port wine. After dinner serve with the coffee two or three kinds of liqueurs. The coffee for dinner parties should be the best quality of Mocha."

During Mr. Roosevelt's time there was a wine cellar at Springwood, to which he carried a key and from which he issued the wines to be served. After his death Mrs. Roosevelt still kept a few wines on hand—Madeira, sherry, claret, and others—which were served as occasion demanded. Then, as today, wines were a necessary accompaniment to the best European cooking.

FISH BALLS, p. 159

A comparison of Mrs. Hitch's recipe with the original in Miss Parloa's *New Cook Book* indicates that the former's version is somewhat simplified, and probably for the better. Miss Parloa calls these "Dropped Fish Balls" and adds, "These balls are delicious." Butter "half the size of an egg" would measure 2 tablespoons or ⅛ cup.

GINGERSNAPS, p. 160

About 4 cups of flour would make this dough very stiff.

RASPBERRY WATER ICE, p. 163

For 4 quarts raspberries, 4 cups sugar and 4 cups (1 quart) water would be today's measurements. Rosa's recipe will be improved with the addition of lemon juice to taste.

DEVONSHIRE PUDDING, p. 164

1 cup bread crumbs, and ¼ cup butter, 1 cup milk, and 1 teaspoonful sugar are proper quantities. A 375° oven would be about right. And strawberry or raspberry jam would be wonderful.

GINGER PUDDING, p. 164

This fine English recipe stands by itself. A pudding steamer or a large tin can (no. 10) might be an improvement over Bessie's basin. A custard sauce is called for in combination with this pudding. Fannie Farmer gives the following:

"2 cups scalded milk   ¼ cup sugar
3 egg yolks   ⅛ teaspoon salt
½ teaspoon vanilla

Beat eggs slightly with fork, add sugar and salt. Add milk gradually stirring constantly. Cook and stir in double boiler until mixture coats the spoon. Strain, chill and flavor. Serves 4. If custard curdles from overcooking, beat with egg beater to restore smoothness."

RUM OR WINE JELLY, p. 165

One strategic detail is lacking—Julie Weiss does not say how much rum or wine is to be added. Fannie Farmer advises 2 cups sherry or Madeira for 4 cups (1 quart) water.

One large cup sugar could well be extended to 2 cups here. One package gelatin is assumed to contain 4 tablespoons.

APPLE BAVAROIS, p. 165

One quart sliced apples would be sufficient—and somewhat less gelatin. Three tablespoons should be enough. Today's cooks do not favor using gelatin just as it comes from the package, but usually soak it (2 tablespoons gelatin to 3 tablespoons water) and then dissolve in 3 tablespoons boiling water, before adding to fruit. This would obviate the necessity of cooking the sugar and gelatin and apples well. If apples are cooked until soft, sugar is stirred in, then gelatin, and the mixture is allowed to remain on the stove just until all ingredients are well blended, better results will be obtained.

WHORTLEBERRY GRIDDLE CAKES, p. 167

"Flour enough to make a nice batter" might read 1½ to 2 cups. Whortleberries being somewhat of a rarity these days, blueberries might be substituted.

SQUASH PIE, p. 167

Again, "butter the size of an egg" translates to ¼ cup butter; and "warmed" should read "melted."

BUCKWHEAT CAKES, p. 171

Homemade liquid yeast was often used in the days before commercial yeast cakes were available. The 1 tablespoon of yeast here may be read ½ yeast cake dissolved in ½ cup warm water.

CORNBREAD, p. 172

Baking cornbread calls for an oven preheated to 425°, and a baking time, at that temperature, of 25 to 30 minutes.

MOLASSES PUDDING, p. 173

The molasses, milk, eggs, and spices should be stirred, of course, into a mixture, which is then poured over the buttered slices of bread, the whole being allowed to soak for an hour. The pudding should be baked in a slow oven—300° for 2 hours.

TO PRESERVE TOMATOES, p. 174

Two handfuls of salt to an undetermined quantity of tomatoes must have produced strange results. Today nearly everyone uses the hot water bath or modern pressure cooker for such operations. The recipe for these methods requires 1 teaspoon of salt to every quart of canned tomatoes.

GINGER SNAPS, p. 174

Although she was obviously fond of gingersnaps, since this is the second recipe for them in the Household Book, Mrs. Roosevelt did not include directions for the famous Algonac ginger snaps as made by her sister, Mrs. Hitch. This recipe, given below, has been kindly furnished for *The House at Hyde Park* by Mrs. Alexander Grant, Mrs. Hitch's niece, daughter of Mr. Frederic A. Delano.

1½ pints molasses (3 cups)   ½ cup water
 6 oz. sugar (about 1⅛ cups) ¼ lb. butter or chicken fat
 ¼ lb. lard or Crisco (½ cup) 3 tablespoons ground ginger
 A little *each* of ground cloves, nutmeg, allspice, cinnamon,
and salt
 1 teaspoon soda
About a pound (3 cups) flour. Use your judgment, as the
dough must not be too hard. Beat the mixture well from the
beginning. Roll the dough very thick, cut out snaps, and
bake on flat buttered tins in a moderate (350°) oven.

CAFÉ MOUSSE, p. 175

Bringing this recipe down to modern possibilities, quantities might read: 1 cup black coffee, yolks of 3 eggs, ¾ cup
sugar, 1 pint heavy cream. Modern cooks will not need to
place in a form packed in ice and salt, but will use the freezing trays of their refrigerators.

MERINGUES, p. 175

Harriet Wood's recipe, p. 146, is superior to this.

CALF'S HEAD AND LIVER, p. 176

Mrs. Roosevelt thought highly of this dish, as there are
three recipes in the Household Book for it; but, modern
taste being what it is, modern cookbooks have little or nothing to say on the subject. All of the recipes sound tasty, if
you like calf's head.

MONT BLANC, p. 177

Fannie Farmer gives quantities as 3 cups boiled mashed chestnuts, sweetened to taste, moistened with a little hot milk, and cooked three minutes. She remarks that it "should look like a mountain."

BRANDY PEACHES, p. 177

The recipe obviously calls for quart jars.

CLAM BROTH, p. 179

Fannie Farmer advocates serving this with salted whipped cream.

PAN DOWDY, p. 181

Miss Parker's recipe for this dessert, on p. 185, will be found superior to the one from Mrs. Lawrence. "Cream of tartar paste" is what we know as baking powder biscuit dough, or shortcake dough. Fannie Farmer gives a good recipe, as follows:

"2 cups flour
4 teaspoons baking powder
½ teaspoon salt

1 tablespoon sugar
¾ cup milk
¼ to 1/3 c butter

Mix dry ingredients, sift twice, work in butter with fork or finger tips, and add milk gradually."

The quantity of apples for Miss Parker's Pan Dowdy should read 4 cups, sliced. One-half cup brown sugar, and ½ cup molasses will be sufficient sweetening, with ½ cup water, ½ teaspoonful each of ground cinnamon and allspice. One hour in a 300° oven should be long enough to cook the apples very soft. The special feature of a pan dowdy is that the crust is broken and stirred into the apples, and then baked, as Miss Parker says, until it is absorbed.

LOBSTER A LA NEWBURG, p. 182

This recipe will call for four pounds of lobster, boiled, of course, before it is added to the melted butter.

MUSHROOMS, p. 182

One pound of mushrooms, 5 tablespoons butter, and 1 cup thin cream may be used here. "A *little* cornstarch" will be about a teaspoonful, although 2 tablespoons of flour may well be substituted for this commodity. Mrs. Sturgis says nothing about slicing the mushrooms, so one presumes they were cooked whole, the caps separated from the stems.

"NOUILLES" OR MACARONI, p. 183

The standard quantities in cooking macaroni are ¾ cup macaroni to 2 quarts boiling water, and 1 tablespoon salt. The oven will need to be heated to 375°, and baking time should be more than slight, for the cheese should be melted —about ten minutes.

SPICE CAKE, p. 187

Mrs. Pell's spice cake should take about 40 minutes in a 350° oven.

DISH MADE OF BOILED FISH, p. 192

This recipe sounds as if boiled halibut might be the main ingredient. It is a good idea to tie the fish in a cloth before immersing in boiling water, and simmer in just enough water to cover, with 1 tablespoon vinegar or lemon juice. Twelve minutes' simmering to the pound is the rule. To get a cupful (Mrs. Roosevelt's half-pint) of béchamel sauce, melt 2 tablespoons butter, stir in until blended 1½ to 2 tablespoons flour, and add slowly ½ cup hot milk and ½ cup of stock in which fish was boiled. Cook and stir until smooth and boiling.

ENTREE DISH FOR LUNCH, p. 197

"Make puff paste" is not quite as simple as it sounds, and since nowhere in the Household Book is a recipe given for this once popular dough, it might be of interest to learn what Miss Parloa has to say on the subject. Her directions, incidentally, agree with the best modern practice. "One quart of pastry flour, one pint of butter, one tablespoonful of salt, one of sugar, one and a quarter cupfuls of ice water. Wash the hands with soap and water, and dip them first in very hot, and then in cold, water. Rinse a large bowl or pan with boiling water and then with cold. Half fill it with cold water. Wash the butter in this, working it with the hands until it is light and waxy. This frees it of the salt and butter-milk and lightens it, so that the pastry is more delicate. Shape the butter in two thin cakes and put in a pan of ice water to harden. Mix the salt and sugar with the flour. With the hands, rub one-third of the butter into the flour. Add the water, stirring with a knife. Stir quickly and vigorously until the paste is a smooth ball. Sprinkle the board *lightly* with flour. Turn the paste on this, and pound quickly and lightly with the rolling pin. Do not break the paste. Roll from you and to one side; or, if easier to roll from you all the while, turn the paste around. When it is about one-fourth of an inch thick wipe the remaining butter, break it in bits and spread these on the paste. Sprinkle lightly with flour. Fold the paste, one-third from each side, so that the edges meet. Now fold from the ends, but do not have these meet. Double the paste, pound lightly and roll down to about one-third of an inch in thickness. Fold as before, and roll down again. Repeat this three times if for pies and six times if for *vol-au-vents,* patties, tarts, etc. Place on the ice to harden, when it has been rolled the last time. It should be in the ice chest at least an hour before being used. In hot weather if the paste sticks when being rolled down put it on a tin sheet and place on ice. As soon as it is chilled it will roll easily. The less flour you use in rolling out the paste the tenderer it will be. No matter how carefully every part of the work may be done, the paste will not be good if much flour is used."

THIN BISCUITS, p. 202

Ten minutes in a 400° oven should be the baking time.

WHEAT BRAN MUFFINS, p. 204

Bake these 40 minutes in a 375° oven.

RISOTTO, p. 205

This is a fine version. Translating into today's measurements, it may be helpful to remember that one pound of butter equals two cups, and one half-ounce equals one tablespoon.

SCOTCH SHORT BREAD, p. 205

Better results will be obtained if baking powder is added to this recipe. Fannie Farmer suggests:

"1 cup butter 　　　　　2 cups bread flour
½ cup confectioner's sugar 　　¼ teaspoon baking powder
¼ teaspoon salt.

Wash butter, add sugar gradually and flour sifted with baking powder and salt. Roll ⅓ inch thick, prick with fork, cut in squares, and bake 20 to 25 minutes in 350° oven, or until delicately brown."

APPLE SAUCE CAKE, p. 211

The method of mixing is to cream butter, add sugar gradually. Add the soda to the apple sauce, and add to butter and sugar. Add other ingredients and bake in a buttered and floured pan 40 minutes at 350°.

FRUIT PUNCH, p. 215

A superlative punch. The banana and cucumber give it really exceptional flavor.

Afterword and Acknowledgments

The reason behind the writing of *The House at Hyde Park* should be made clear, if this volume is to fulfill its purpose.

The Hyde Park Free Library, built as a memorial to James Roosevelt by his widow Sara, was given financial assistance by her during her lifetime. After her death her son, Franklin, continued to make up library deficits. In 1947 his heirs sold it to the town of Hyde Park. Since that date, the question of funds necessary to keep it running has steadily become more acute.

Wishing to help in this difficulty, Mr. Herman Kahn, Director of the Franklin D. Roosevelt Library, a branch of the Archives of the United States, released Sara Roosevelt's Household Book from the Roosevelt Family Papers for the use of the Hyde Park Free Library.

The authors, believing that free public libraries are essential to democratic American communities, offered to supplement the Household Book with their own research and writing about Franklin D. Roosevelt's father and mother. In order to implement their convictions, they have stipulated that all royalties from the sale of this book, over and above the original editorial costs, be given to the Hyde Park Free Library, a community enterprise.

As for acknowledgments, so many people have been good enough to help in the preparation of *The House at Hyde Park* that it is difficult to know where to begin in any expression of gratitude. Perhaps the first vote of thanks should go to the residents of Hyde Park, who were unfailingly helpful and courteous to the authors, and who have followed the progress of the book with friendly interest. These include Mr. Benjamin Haviland (whom Franklin Roosevelt called "Uncle Ben"); Dr. James M. Cronk, family physician to his neighbors in Hyde Park for more than fifty years; Mr. Moses Smith, superintendent of Franklin Roosevelt's own farm, and Mrs. Smith; their son Mr. Arthur Smith, postmaster at Hyde Park; Miss Evaretta Killmer, one of the original members of Mrs. Roosevelt's sewing class; Mr. John Clay, who hung much of the wallpaper in the house at Hyde Park; Mr. Angus Brownell, who with his wife came down from Canada to make butter at Mrs. Roosevelt's farm; and Mr. Charles Van Curen; his daughter, Miss Alma Van Curen; Mr. Frank Drais; Mr. Raymond O'Dell; Mr. and Mrs. Robert McGaughey; Mr. and Mrs. Louis De Pew, formerly associated with the Roosevelt home and farm, and to-day employed at Hyde Park by the United States Government. Mr. and Mrs. William Plog deserve special thanks for allowing the authors to interfere with the pursuits of their busy life. After more than fifty years in the Roosevelt gardens and greenhouses, Mr. Plog still exerts the magic of his green thumb for the house at Hyde Park.

Others who have taken of their time and energy to be helpful are:

Dr. Wirt C. Groom, Acting Senior Director of the Hudson River State Hospital

Mr. Olaf Johnson, Secretary-Treasurer of the New Industries Bureau of Superior, Wisconsin

Mr. W. H. Higinbotham, Assistant Secretary of the Delaware and Hudson Company

Mr. Frederic A. Wyatt, Director of Alumnae Relations, Union College

Mrs. Edith P. Newton, Registrar of the Law School of Harvard University

Miss Eileen Thornton, Librarian, and Miss Elizabeth Richards, Reference Librarian, of the Vassar College Library

Miss Albertina T. B. Traver and Mrs. Amy Ver Nooy of the Adriance Library, Poughkeepsie, New York

To Mrs. Theodore Douglas Robinson, granddaughter of James Roosevelt, the authors express their gratitude for help and kindness.

To Miss Ellen C. Roosevelt, niece of James Roosevelt, they are indebted for permission to visit Rosedale, and for many interesting family anecdotes.

To Mrs. Rita Halle Kleeman, personal friend of Sara Roosevelt and pioneer in biographical writing about the Roosevelt family, the authors pay their cordial respects. They acknowledge their indebtedness to her and her publishers, Appleton-Century-Crofts, Inc., for permission to quote from original sources used in her book, *Gracious Lady,* and to incorporate such material in this book.

And finally, to Mrs. James Lawrence Houghteling and Mrs. Alexander Grant, nieces of Mrs. James Roosevelt, the authors wish to extend their heartiest thanks for truly significant help.

CLARA AND HARDY STEEHOLM

Salt Point
Dutchess County
New York

GENERAL INDEX

INDEX OF THE
HOUSEHOLD BOOK

General Index

265

Index of the Household Book